NO FEAR SHAKESPEARE

NO FEAR SHAKESPEARE

As You Like It

The Comedy of Errors

Hamlet

Henry IV, Parts One and Two

Henry V

Julius Caesar

King Lear

Macbeth

The Merchant of Venice

A Midsummer Night's Dream

Much Ado About Nothing

Othello

Richard III

Romeo and Juliet

Sonnets

The Taming of the Shrew

The Tempest

Twelfth Night

NO FEAR SHAKESPEARE

MUCH ADO ABOUT NOTHING

The original text and translation for this edition was prepared by John Crowther.

Spark Publishing
A Division of Barnes & Noble, Inc.
120 Fifth Avenue
New York, NY 10011
www.sparknotes.com

Please submit all comments and questions or report errors to www.sparknotes.com/errors

ISBN: 978-1-4114-0101-3

Printed and bound in the United States of America

40 39 38 37

There's matter in these sighs, these profound heaves.
You must translate: 'tis fit we understand them.

(*Hamlet*, 4.1.1–2)

FEAR NOT.

Have you ever found yourself looking at a Shakespeare play, then down at the footnotes, then back at the play, and still not understanding? You know what the individual words mean, but they don't add up. SparkNotes' *No Fear Shakespeare* will help you break through all that. Put the pieces together with our easy-to-read translations. Soon you'll be reading Shakespeare's own words fearlessly—and actually enjoying it.

No Fear Shakespeare puts Shakespeare's language side-by-side with a facing-page translation into modern English— the kind of English people actually speak today. When Shakespeare's words make your head spin, our translation will help you sort out what's happening, who's saying what, and why.

MUCH ADO ABOUT NOTHING

Characters ix

CHARACTERS

Beatrice—The niece of Leonato and cousin of Hero. Beatrice is extremely quick-witted and verbally adept, frequently amusing her relatives and friends with elaborate stories and jokes, often at her own expense. Though she is generous and good-hearted, she has a tendency to use her wit to mock and tease other people. Benedick is the target of her harshest mockery.

Benedick—A gentleman soldier who has recently been fighting under Don Pedro, and a close friend of Don Pedro and Claudio. Like Beatrice, Benedick is very witty and fond of mocking other people with elaborate jokes, comparisons, and puns. He swears he will never marry, as he is very critical of women and does not trust any of them not to cheat on him.

Claudio—A young soldier who has won great acclaim fighting under Don Pedro during the recent wars. Claudio falls in love with Hero upon his return to Messina. Though he is valiant and loving, he is unfortunately gullible, quick to believe nasty rumors and to feel that he's been betrayed by those close to him.

Hero—The beautiful young daughter of Leonato, and cousin to Beatrice. Hero is lovely, gentle, and innocent.

Don Pedro—A very important nobleman from Aragon, often referred to simply as "the Prince." Don Pedro is a longtime friend of Leonato, Hero's father, and is also close to the soldiers who have been fighting under him—the younger Benedick and the very young Claudio. Don Pedro is generous, courteous, intelligent, and loving to his friends, but he is also quick to believe evil of others and hasty to take revenge. He is the most politically and socially powerful character in the play.

Leonato—The father of Hero and the uncle of Beatrice. Leonato is the governor of Messina and a respected, well-to-do, elderly nobleman. The action of the play takes place in his home. Leonato is second in status only to Don Pedro.

Don John—Don Pedro's illegitimate half brother, sometimes referred to simply as "the Bastard." Don John is melancholy and sullen by nature, and he creates a dark scheme to ruin the happiness of Hero and Claudio. He is the villain of the play, his evil actions motivated mainly by his envy of his brother's power and authority.

Margaret—Hero's serving woman, who unwittingly helps Borachio and Don John deceive Claudio into thinking that Hero is unfaithful. Unlike Ursula, Hero's other lady-in-waiting, Margaret is lower class. Though she is honest, she does have some dealings with the villainous world of Don John: her lover is the mistrustful and easily bribed Borachio. Also unlike Ursula, Margaret loves to break decorum, especially with bawdy jokes and teasing.

Borachio—An associate of Don John, and the lover of Margaret, Hero's serving woman. Borachio conspires with Don John to trick Claudio and Don Pedro into thinking that Hero is unfaithful to Claudio. His name means "drunkard" in Italian.

Conrad—One of Don John's intimate associates, entirely devoted to Don John and his schemes.

Dogberry—The chief policeman of Messina, in charge of the watch. Dogberry is very sincere and takes his job seriously, but he has a habit of using exactly the wrong word to convey his meaning. Dogberry is one of the few middle-class characters in the play, though his desire to speak formally and elaborately like the noblemen becomes an occasion for parody.

Verges—The deputy to Dogberry, chief policeman of Messina.

Antonio—Leonato's elderly brother, and Hero and Beatrice's uncle.

Balthasar—A waiting man in Leonato's household, and a musician. Balthasar flirts with Margaret at the masked party and helps Leonato, Claudio, and Don Pedro trick Benedick into falling in love with Beatrice. Balthasar sings the song "Sigh no more, ladies, sigh no more," which encourages women to accept men's infidelity as natural.

Ursula—One of Hero's waiting women.

NO FEAR SHAKESPEARE

MUCH ADO ABOUT NOTHING

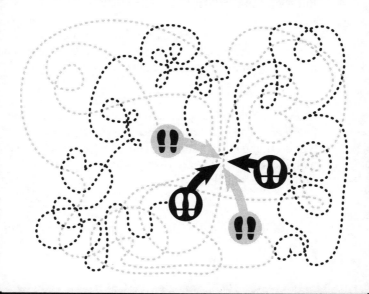

ACT ONE
SCENE 1

Enter LEONATO, *Governor of Messina;* HERO, *his daughter;*
and BEATRICE *his niece, with a* MESSENGER

LEONATO
> I learn in this letter that Don Pedro of Aragon comes this
> night to Messina.

MESSENGER
> He is very near by this. He was not three leagues off when
> I left him.

LEONATO
> How many gentlemen have you lost in this action?

MESSENGER
> But few of any sort, and none of name.

LEONATO
> A victory is twice itself when the achiever brings home full
> numbers. I find here that Don Pedro hath bestowed much
> honor on a young Florentine called Claudio.

MESSENGER
> Much deserved on his part, and equally remembered by
> Don Pedro. He hath borne himself beyond the promise of
> his age, doing in the figure of a lamb the feats of a lion. He
> hath indeed better bettered expectation than you must
> expect of me to tell you how.

LEONATO
> He hath an uncle here in Messina will be very much glad of
> it.

ACT ONE
SCENE 1

LEONATO, *Governor of Messina;* HERO, *his daughter; and* BEATRICE, *his niece, enter with a* MESSENGER

LEONATO

"Don" is the Italian equivalent of "Sir" or "Lord."

(holding a letter) According to this letter, Don Pedro of Aragon and his army are coming to Messina tonight.

MESSENGER

He must be very near by now. When I left him, he was less than nine miles from here.

LEONATO

How many noblemen were killed in the battle you just fought?

MESSENGER

Not many, and no one important.

LEONATO

A victory in battle is twice as victorious when all the soldiers return home safely. This letter also says that Don Pedro has given honors to a young man from Florence named Claudio.

MESSENGER

Claudio deserves to be honored, and Don Pedro has rewarded him accordingly. Claudio has done more than anyone would expect of a man his age. He looks like a lamb but fights like a lion. He has so greatly exceeded all expectations that I can't even describe all he's done.

LEONATO

He has an uncle here in Messina who will be glad to hear this news.

MESSENGER
I have already delivered him letters, and there appears
much joy in him—even so much that joy could not show
itself modest enough without a badge of bitterness.

LEONATO
20   Did he break out into tears?

MESSENGER
In great measure.

LEONATO
A kind overflow of kindness. There are no faces truer than
those that are so washed. How much better is it to weep at
joy than to joy at weeping!

BEATRICE
25   I pray you, is Signor Montanto returned from the wars or
no?

MESSENGER
I know none of that name, lady. There was none such in the
army of any sort.

LEONATO
What is he that you ask for, niece?

HERO
30   My cousin means Signor Benedick of Padua.

MESSENGER
Oh, he's returned, and as pleasant as ever he was.

BEATRICE
He set up his bills here in Messina and challenged Cupid at
the flight, and my uncle's Fool, reading the challenge,
subscribed for Cupid and challenged him at the bird-bolt.
35   I pray you, how many hath he killed and eaten in these
wars? But how many hath he killed? For indeed I promised
to eat all of his killing.

MESSENGER

I have delivered some letters to his uncle, and he seemed very happy. He got so emotional that he actually looked like he was in pain.

LEONATO

Did he start weeping?

MESSENGER

Yes, heavily.

LEONATO

That's a very natural display of affection. There's no face more sincere than one washed in tears. And it's definitely better to cry because you're happy than laugh because you're sad!

BEATRICE

"Montanto" is a fencing term for an upward thrust.

Please tell me, has Signior Montanto returned from battle?

MESSENGER

I don't know anyone with that name, ma'am. There was no Signior Montanto in our army.

LEONATO

Who are you talking about, niece?

HERO

My cousin means Signior Benedick of Padua.

MESSENGER

Oh, yes, Benedick has returned and is as cheerful as ever.

BEATRICE

The exact meaning of this story is unclear, but it depicts Benedick as a braggart and a fool.

Benedick once put up a public notice in Messina challenging Cupid to an archery match. My uncle's jester accepted the contest on Cupid's behalf but used toy arrows at the shooting match. But tell me, how many men did he kill and eat in this battle? I promised him I would eat anyone he killed.

LEONATO

Faith, niece, you tax Signor Benedick too much, but he'll be
meet with you, I doubt it not.

MESSENGER

40   He hath done good service, lady, in these wars.

BEATRICE

You had musty victual, and he hath holp to eat it. He is a
very valiant trencherman. He hath an excellent stomach.

MESSENGER

And a good soldier too, lady.

BEATRICE

And a good soldier to a lady, but what is he to a lord?

MESSENGER

45   A lord to a lord, a man to a man, stuffed with all honorable
virtues.

BEATRICE

It is so indeed. He is no less than a stuffed man. But for the
stuffing—well, we are all mortal.

LEONATO

You must not, sir, mistake my niece. There is a kind of
50   merry war betwixt Signor Benedick and her. They never
meet but there's a skirmish of wit between them.

BEATRICE

Alas, he gets nothing by that. In our last conflict four of his
five wits went halting off, and now is the whole man
governed with one, so that if he have wit enough to keep
55   himself warm, let him bear it for a difference between
himself and his horse, for it is all the wealth that he hath left
to be known a reasonable creature. Who is his companion
now? He hath every month a new sworn brother.

MESSENGER

Is 't possible?

LEONATO

For God's sake, Beatrice, you're criticizing Signior Benedick too heavily. But I'm sure he'll get even with you.

MESSENGER

Signior Benedick served well in the war, my lady.

BEATRICE

You had rotten food, and he helped you eat it. He's a very brave eater—he has a strong stomach.

MESSENGER

He's a good soldier too, lady.

BEATRICE

He's a good soldier to a lady? Well then, what is he to a lord?

MESSENGER

He's a lord to a lord and a man to a man. He is positively stuffed with honorable virtues.

BEATRICE

Absolutely—he is stuffed, like a dummy. As for what he's stuffed with—well, nobody's perfect.

LEONATO

Please don't take my niece the wrong way, sir. Benedick and Beatrice have been waging a war of wits between themselves. Whenever they meet, there's a little battle.

BEATRICE

And I always win. The last time we fought, he was so dazed by the end that he wasn't much smarter than his horse. So tell me, who is he hanging around with these days? Every month he has a new best friend.

MESSENGER

Is that possible?

BEATRICE

60 Very easily possible. He wears his faith but as the fashion of
his hat; it ever changes with the next block.

MESSENGER

I see, lady, the gentleman is not in your books.

BEATRICE

No. An he were, I would burn my study. But I pray you,
who is his companion? Is there no young squarer now that
65 will make a voyage with him to the devil?

MESSENGER

He is most in the company of the right noble Claudio.

BEATRICE

O Lord, he will hang upon him like a disease! He is sooner
caught than the pestilence, and the taker runs presently
mad. God help the noble Claudio! If he have caught the
70 Benedick, it will cost him a thousand pound ere a be cured.

MESSENGER

I will hold friends with you, lady.

BEATRICE

Do, good friend.

LEONATO

You will never run mad, niece.

BEATRICE

No, not till a hot January.

MESSENGER

75 Don Pedro is approached.

Enter DON PEDRO, *Prince of Aragon, with* CLAUDIO,
BENEDICK, BALTHASAR, *and* DON JOHN *the bastard*

DON PEDRO

Good Signor Leonato, are you come to meet your trouble?
The fashion of the world is to avoid cost, and you encounter
it.

BEATRICE

It's entirely possible. He's incredibly fickle—his affection changes faster than the latest fashions.

MESSENGER

I can see you don't like this gentleman.

BEATRICE

No, absolutely not. But please tell me, who's his best friend? Isn't there some new swaggering young ruffian who will happily go to hell with Benedick?

MESSENGER

He spends most of his time with the good, noble Claudio.

BEATRICE

Oh God, Benedick will plague him like a disease! Benedick is an infection that's easy to catch but hard to get rid of—and he'll drive you crazy once you've been infected. God help Claudio! If he's caught the Benedick, he'll lose all his money before he's cured.

MESSENGER

I'm going to make sure I stay on your good side, lady.

BEATRICE

Do that, my friend.

LEONATO

You will never fall victim to Benedick's charms, my niece.

BEATRICE

No, not until we see a hot January.

MESSENGER

Don Pedro is here.

Don John is Don Pedro's illegitimate half-brother.

DON PEDRO, *Prince of Aragon, enters with* **CLAUDIO**, **BENEDICK**, **BALTHASAR**, *and* **DON JOHN**, *the bastard.*

DON PEDRO

My dear Signior Leonato, hosting my whole army is such a huge burden, but you accept it—and me—with open arms. Most people choose to avoid trouble, but you run to it.

LEONATO
> Never came trouble to my house in the likeness of your
80 > Grace, for trouble being gone, comfort should remain, but
> when you depart from me, sorrow abides and happiness
> takes his leave.

DON PEDRO
> You embrace your charge too willingly. I think this is your
> daughter.

LEONATO
85 > Her mother hath many times told me so.

BENEDICK
> Were you in doubt, sir, that you asked her?

LEONATO
> Signor Benedick, no, for then were you a child.

DON PEDRO
> You have it full, Benedick. We may guess by this what you
> are, being a man. Truly, the lady fathers herself.—Be
90 > happy, lady, for you are like an honorable father.

LEONATO and DON PEDRO move to one side, still talking

BENEDICK
> If Signor Leonato be her father, she would not have his
> head on her shoulders for all Messina, as like him as she is.

BEATRICE
> I wonder that you will still be talking, Signor Benedick.
> Nobody marks you.

BENEDICK
95 > What, my dear Lady Disdain! Are you yet living?

LEONATO

You are never trouble to this house, your Grace. It's comforting when trouble departs. But when *you* leave, you take happiness with you and leave sorrow in its place.

DON PEDRO

You take up your duties too cheerfully. *(turning to* HERO*)* This must be your daughter.

LEONATO

That's what her mother always tells me.

BENEDICK

Did you doubt that she was your daughter, since you had to ask her mother?

LEONATO

(teasing) Of course not, Signior Benedick. You were only a child when my daughter was born, and not yet old enough to seduce my wife.

DON PEDRO

Ah, he got you back, Benedick! Leonato clearly knows your reputation with women. Seriously, though, the lady resembles Leonato so much that there can be no doubt about who her father is. Congratulations, lady: you resemble a most honorable man.

LEONATO *and* DON PEDRO *move to one side, still talking.*

BENEDICK

Well, even if he is her father, I'm sure she wouldn't want to have the head of the old man on her shoulders!

BEATRICE

I'm amazed you're still talking, Signior Benedick. No one's listening to you.

BENEDICK

Look, it's my dear Lady Disdain! Aren't you dead yet?

BEATRICE

Is it possible disdain should die while she hath such meet
food to feed it as Signor Benedick? Courtesy itself must
convert to disdain if you come in her presence.

BENEDICK

Then is courtesy a turncoat. But it is certain I am loved of
100   all ladies, only you excepted. And I would I could find in
my heart that I had not a hard heart, for truly I love none.

BEATRICE

A dear happiness to women. They would else have been
troubled with a pernicious suitor. I thank God and my cold
blood I am of your humor for that. I had rather hear my dog
105   bark at a crow than a man swear he loves me.

BENEDICK

God keep your Ladyship still in that mind, so some gentleman or other shall 'scape a predestinate scratched face.

BEATRICE

Scratching could not make it worse an 'twere such a face as
yours were.

BENEDICK

110   Well, you are a rare parrot-teacher.

BEATRICE

A bird of my tongue is better than a beast of yours.

BENEDICK

I would my horse had the speed of your tongue and so good
a continuer. But keep your way, i' God's name. I have done.

BEATRICE

You always end with a jade's trick. I know you of old.

LEONATO *and* DON PEDRO *come forward*

DON PEDRO

115   That is the sum of all, Leonato.—Signior Claudio and
Signior Benedick, my dear friend Leonato hath invited you
all. I tell him we shall stay here at the least a month, and he
heartily prays some occasion may detain us longer. I dare
swear he is no hypocrite but prays from his heart.

BEATRICE

How could disdain die when you're here? When you're around, even Lady Courtesy becomes Lady Disdain.

BENEDICK

That makes Lady Courtesy a traitor. All ladies love me, except you. It's too bad I'm so hard-hearted, because I really don't love anyone.

BEATRICE

Women are lucky, then. You would make a nasty suitor. Thankfully, I feel the same way you do. I have no need for romance. I would rather listen to my dog bark at a crow than hear a man swear that he loves me.

BENEDICK

Well, I hope you stay in that frame of mind or some poor man will end up with his face all scratched up.

BEATRICE

If he has a face like yours, a good scratching couldn't make him look any worse.

BENEDICK

Listen to you, instructing me like a parrot would.

BEATRICE

I'd rather be a squawking bird than an animal like you.

BENEDICK

I wish my horse moved as fast as your mouth and was as tireless. That's it—I'm done.

BEATRICE

You always slip out of the argument like this. I know you from before.

LEONATO *and* DON PEDRO *come forward*

DON PEDRO

And that's everything, Leonato.—Claudio, Benedick—my dear friend Leonato has invited you all to stay here at Messina. I told him we'll stay for at least a month, and he says that he hopes we'll stay longer. I think he's actually serious, and not just being polite.

LEONATO

120   If you swear, my lord, you shall not be forsworn. *(to* DON
        JOHN*)* Let me bid you welcome, my lord. Being reconciled
        to the Prince your brother, I owe you all duty.

DON JOHN

        I thank you. I am not of many words, but I thank you.

LEONATO

        Please it your Grace lead on?

DON PEDRO

125   Your hand, Leonato. We will go together.

                    Exeunt. Manent BENEDICK *and* CLAUDIO

CLAUDIO

        Benedick, didst thou note the daughter of Signior Leonato?

BENEDICK

        I noted her not, but I looked on her.

CLAUDIO

        Is she not a modest young lady?

BENEDICK

        Do you question me as an honest man should do, for my
130   simple true judgment? Or would you have me speak after
        my custom, as being a professed tyrant to their sex?

CLAUDIO

        No, I pray thee speak in sober judgment.

BENEDICK

        Why, i' faith, methinks she's too low for a high praise, too
        brown for a fair praise, and too little for a great praise. Only
135   this commendation I can afford her, that were she other
        than she is, she were unhandsome, and being no other but
        as she is, I do not like her.

CLAUDIO

        Thou thinkest I am in sport. I pray thee tell me truly how
        thou lik'st her.

LEONATO

> I am being serious, my lord. *(to* DON JOHN*)* I welcome you here as well. Now that you and your brother have made friends again, I owe you the same allegiance I owe Don Pedro.

DON JOHN

> Thank you. I'm not a man who talks a lot, but I thank you.

LEONATO

> If it pleases you, your highness, will you lead us all inside?

DON PEDRO

> Give me your hand, Leonato. We will go in together.

> *Everyone exits except* BENEDICK *and* CLAUDIO.

CLAUDIO

> Benedick, did you notice Signior Leonato's daughter?

BENEDICK

> I saw her, but I didn't notice her.

CLAUDIO

> Isn't she a well-mannered young lady?

BENEDICK

> Do you want my true opinion? Or do you want me to criticize her like I do all women?

CLAUDIO

> No, please, speak seriously.

BENEDICK

> Well, it seems to me that she is too short to be praised highly, too dark to be praised fairly, and too small to be praised greatly. I can only say this about her: if she looked different than she does, she would be ugly, and since she can't be anything but herself, I don't like her.

CLAUDIO

> You think I'm kidding. Please tell me seriously what you think of her.

BENEDICK

140   Would you buy her, that you enquire after her?

CLAUDIO

     Can the world buy such a jewel?

BENEDICK

     Yea, and a case to put it into. But speak you this with a sad
     brow? Or do you play the flouting jack, to tell us Cupid is
     a good hare-finder and Vulcan a rare carpenter? Come, in
145   what key shall a man take you to go in the song?

CLAUDIO

     In mine eye she is the sweetest lady that ever I looked on.

BENEDICK

     I can see yet without spectacles, and I see no such matter.
     There's her cousin, an she were not possessed with a fury,
     exceeds her as much in beauty as the first of May doth the
150   last of December. But I hope you have no intent to turn
     husband, have you?

CLAUDIO

     I would scarce trust myself, though I had sworn the
     contrary, if Hero would be my wife.

BENEDICK

     Is 't come to this? In faith, hath not the world one man but
155   he will wear his cap with suspicion? Shall I never see a
     bachelor of three-score again? Go to, i' faith, an thou wilt
     needs thrust thy neck into a yoke, wear the print of it, and
     sigh away Sundays. Look, Don Pedro is returned to seek
     you.

Enter **DON PEDRO**

BENEDICK

Are you thinking of buying her? Is that why you're asking?

CLAUDIO

Would it even be possible to buy a jewel as rare and precious as Hero?

BENEDICK

Yes, and you could buy a case to put it in, too. But tell me, are you speaking seriously? Or are you just teasing? If I'm going to sing along with you, I need to know what key you're singing in.

CLAUDIO

I think she's the most wonderful woman I've ever laid eyes on.

BENEDICK

I'm still young enough to see without glasses, and I don't see what you're talking about. If her cousin Beatrice didn't have such a nasty temper, she'd be so much more beautiful than Hero that it would be like comparing May to December. But, hey, this doesn't mean you're looking to get married, does it?

CLAUDIO

Even if I had sworn never to marry, I wouldn't trust myself to keep that promise if Hero would marry me.

BENEDICK

What's going on these days? Isn't there one man left in the world who knows not to take a wife? She's just going to cheat on him. Will I never see a sixty-year old bachelor again or will all men be swindled into marriage while they're young? Go ahead, then, if you have to yoke yourself to marriage, like an ox carrying his load, and throw away your free time. Look, Don Pedro has come back for you.

DON PEDRO enters.

DON PEDRO
160   What secret hath held you here that you followed not to
        Leonato's?

BENEDICK
        I would your grace would constrain me to tell.

DON PEDRO
        I charge thee on thy allegiance.

BENEDICK
        You hear, Count Claudio? I can be secret as a dumb man, I
165   would have you think so, but on my allegiance—mark you
        this, on my allegiance—*(to* **DON PEDRO***)* he is in love. With
        who? Now, that is your Grace's part. Mark how short his
        answer is: with Hero, Leonato's short daughter.

CLAUDIO
        If this were so, so were it uttered.

BENEDICK
170   Like the old tale, my lord: "It is not so nor 'twas not so but,
        indeed, God forbid it should be so."

CLAUDIO
        If my passion change not shortly, God forbid it should be
        otherwise.

DON PEDRO
        Amen, if you love her, for the lady is very well worthy.

CLAUDIO
175   You speak this to fetch me in, my lord.

DON PEDRO
        By my troth, I speak my thought.

CLAUDIO
        And, in faith, my lord, I spoke mine.

NO FEAR SHAKESPEARE

DON PEDRO

What secrets between you have kept you from following us to Leonato's?

BENEDICK

Your highness will have to force me to tell.

DON PEDRO

Your loyalty to me requires you to tell me what you've been talking about.

BENEDICK

Look, Claudio, I can keep secrets like a mute; I want you to know that. But I owe Don Pedro my allegiance—look, I *have* to tell him—*(to* DON PEDRO*)* Claudio is in love. With whom? That's what you're supposed to ask me next, your Grace. Look how short the answer is—with Hero, Leonato's short daughter.

CLAUDIO

If you say so.

BENEDICK

Listen to him deny it, like that man in the old tale "Mr. Fox": "It isn't true and wasn't true and God forbid it should be so."

CLAUDIO

Unless my feelings change very soon, I have to admit it's true.

DON PEDRO

It's good if you love Hero, because she's worthy of your love.

CLAUDIO

You're trying to trick me, my lord.

DON PEDRO

I swear, I'm telling you what I honestly think.

CLAUDIO

And I swear I spoke honestly to Benedick—I am in love with Hero.

BENEDICK
And by my two faiths and troths, my lord, I spoke mine.

CLAUDIO
That I love her, I feel.

DON PEDRO
180   That she is worthy, I know.

BENEDICK
That I neither feel how she should be loved nor know how she should be worthy is the opinion that fire cannot melt out of me. I will die in it at the stake.

DON PEDRO
Thou wast ever an obstinate heretic in the despite of beauty.

CLAUDIO
185   And never could maintain his part but in the force of his will.

BENEDICK
That a woman conceived me, I thank her. That she brought me up, I likewise give her most humble thanks. But that I will have a recheat winded in my forehead or hang my bugle in an invisible baldrick, all women shall pardon me.
190   Because I will not do them the wrong to mistrust any, I will do myself the right to trust none. And the fine is, for the which I may go the finer, I will live a bachelor.

DON PEDRO
I shall see thee, ere I die, look pale with love.

BENEDICK
With anger, with sickness, or with hunger, my lord, not
195   with love. Prove that ever I lose more blood with love than I will get again with drinking, pick out mine eyes with a ballad-maker's pen and hang me up at the door of a brothel house for the sign of blind Cupid.

BENEDICK

And *I* swear all up and down I spoke honestly when I said that this was a horrible idea.

CLAUDIO

I feel that I love her.

DON PEDRO

I know that she is worthy of that love.

BENEDICK

I, on the other hand, don't *feel* how she could be loved and don't *know* how she could be worthy. Even fire can't melt that opinion out of me. You could burn me at the stake, and I'd still think this.

DON PEDRO

You never did believe in the power of beauty.

CLAUDIO

Or in the power of reason.

BENEDICK

I was conceived by a woman, and I thank her very much for all her effort. And then she brought me up, and I thank her for that, too. But all the other women will have to forgive me for not being willing to be made a fool of—cheated on by a wife. I don't want to insult any particular woman by doubting and mistrusting her, so I'll just avoid them all. And the conclusion of this is that I'll live as a bachelor—and, with the money I save, dress better.

DON PEDRO

I swear, before I die I'm going to see you sick with love.

BENEDICK

With anger, with fever, or with hunger, sure, my friend, but never sick with love. If you can prove that I'll ever be so in love that I can't be brought to my senses with a good round of beers, you can pluck out my eyes with a love-poet's pen and hang me on a brothel's door where the picture of blind Cupid usually goes.

DON PEDRO
Well, if ever thou dost fall from this faith, thou wilt prove
200   a notable argument.

BENEDICK
If I do, hang me in a bottle like a cat and shoot at me, and he
that hits me, let him be clapped on the shoulder and called
Adam.

DON PEDRO
Well, as time shall try.
205   In time the savage bull doth bear the yoke.

BENEDICK
The savage bull may, but if ever the sensible Benedick bear
it, pluck off the bull's horns and set them in my forehead,
and let me be vilely painted, and in such great letters as they
write "Here is good horse to hire" let them signify under my
210   sign "Here you may see Benedick the married man."

CLAUDIO
If this should ever happen, thou wouldst be horn-mad.

DON PEDRO
Nay, if Cupid have not spent all his quiver in Venice, thou
wilt quake for this shortly.

BENEDICK
I look for an earthquake too, then.

DON PEDRO
215   Well, you temporize with the hours. In the meantime, good
Signior Benedick, repair to Leonato's. Commend me to
him and tell him I will not fail him at supper, for indeed he
hath made great preparation.

BENEDICK
I have almost matter enough in me for such an embassage,
220   and so I commit you—

NO FEAR SHAKESPEARE

DON PEDRO

I'll be sure to remember this fuss you've made, in case you ever do fall in love. That'll be news.

BENEDICK

If I ever change my mind, you can use me for target practice. And whoever hits the bull's eye gets to be a hero.

DON PEDRO

Well, time will tell. Even the most savage bull is eventually domesticated.

BENEDICK

A "cuckold" is a man whose wife has cheated on him, and is popularly depicted as a man with horns.

Maybe the bull is, but if *I* am ever domesticated, you can take that bull's horns and put them right on my forehead, as my wife is sure to cuckold me soon enough. You might as well hang a big sign with enormous lettering around my neck. But instead of it saying "Horse for hire," it will say "Take a look at Benedick, the married man."

CLAUDIO

If that ever happened, you'd go absolutely mad.

DON PEDRO

Well, if Cupid hasn't used up all his arrows in Venice, where the courtesans are famous for making men lovesick, he'll get you to quiver and shake. Just you wait.

BENEDICK

That's about as likely as an earthquake.

DON PEDRO

Oh, you'll soften as time passes. While you're waiting for that to happen, though, hurry to Leonato's. Give him my respects, and tell him I'll definitely be there for dinner, since I know he has gone to great lengths for this meal.

BENEDICK

I think I can handle this mission. And so I commit you—

CLAUDIO
To the tuition of God. From my house, if I had it—

DON PEDRO
The sixth of July. Your loving friend, Benedick.

BENEDICK
Nay, mock not, mock not. The body of your discourse is
sometimes guarded with fragments and the guards are but
225   slightly basted on neither. Ere you flout old ends any
further, examine your conscience. And so I leave you.

Exit

CLAUDIO
My liege, your highness now may do me good.

DON PEDRO
My love is thine to teach. Teach it but how,
And thou shalt see how apt it is to learn
230   Any hard lesson that may do thee good.

CLAUDIO
Hath Leonato any son, my lord?

DON PEDRO
No child but Hero; she's his only heir.
Dost thou affect her, Claudio?

CLAUDIO
                  O, my lord,
235   When you went onward on this ended action,
I looked upon her with a soldier's eye,
That liked but had a rougher task in hand
Than to drive liking to the name of love.
But now I am returned and that war thoughts
240   Have left their places vacant, in their rooms
Come thronging soft and delicate desires,
All prompting me how fair young Hero is,
Saying I liked her ere I went to wars.

CLAUDIO

"Into God's hands. From my house, if I had a house—"

DON PEDRO

"The sixth of July. Sincerely, your loving friend, Benedick."

BENEDICK

Benedick and Claudio are making fun of the fact that "I commit you" is, in Shakespeare's time, a common way to end a formal letter.

Oh, stop joking around. You know, sometimes you two dress up your conversation with flimsy little bits of wit that don't hold together too well. Before you make fun of everyone else, look at yourselves in the mirror! And with that, I'm leaving.

He exits.

CLAUDIO

My lord, you could really help me out now.

DON PEDRO

I am at your service. Just tell me what you want me to do, and however hard it is, you'll see that I'm eager to do it.

CLAUDIO

Does Leonato have a son, my lord?

DON PEDRO

Hero is his only child, and his only heir. Do you like her, Claudio?

CLAUDIO

Oh, my lord, when we left Messina to fight the war, I looked at Hero with the eyes of a soldier. I liked what I saw, but my mind was so occupied with the rough, violent task ahead of me that there was no chance that *like* would turn into *love*. But now that I'm back, the room in my head that I used to fill with war plans has become crowded with soft and delicate feelings. They all lead me to the same thought—how beautiful young Hero is and how I must have liked her even before I left to fight.

DON PEDRO
Thou wilt be like a lover presently
245   And tire the hearer with a book of words.
If thou dost love fair Hero, cherish it,
And I will break with her and with her father,
And thou shalt have her. Was 't not to this end
That thou began'st to twist so fine a story?

CLAUDIO
250   How sweetly you do minister to love,
That know love's grief by his complexion!
But lest my liking might too sudden seem,
I would have salved it with a longer treatise.

DON PEDRO
What need the bridge much broader than the flood?
255   The fairest grant is the necessity.
Look what will serve is fit. 'Tis once, thou lovest,
And I will fit thee with the remedy.
I know we shall have reveling tonight.
I will assume thy part in some disguise
260   And tell fair Hero I am Claudio,
And in her bosom I'll unclasp my heart
And take her hearing prisoner with the force
And strong encounter of my amorous tale.
Then after to her father will I break,
265   And the conclusion is, she shall be thine.
In practice let us put it presently.

Exeunt

DON PEDRO

You will become a true lover soon, and exhaust your friends with your endless chatter about your feelings. Look, if you really love the beautiful Hero, enjoy it. I will speak to her and her father about the matter, and I'll convince Leonato to promise Hero to you. Isn't that the reason you told me all this?

CLAUDIO

You can see that I'm sick with love, and you're taking care of me in just the right way! But I didn't want you to think that I'm hasty in my emotions. I was going to explain my feelings with a longer story.

DON PEDRO

Why speak longer than you have to? That's like building a bridge wider than the river it crosses. Whatever gets the job done is best. You love Hero; that's all I need to know to want to find a remedy. They're going to have a costume party with dancing tonight. I'll disguise myself as you and pour out "my" feelings to Hero, taking her prisoner with the force of my love story. Then I'll talk to her father. And in the end, she's yours! Let's get started right away.

They exit.

ACT 1, SCENE 2

Enter LEONATO *and* ANTONIO

LEONATO

How now, brother, where is my cousin, your son? Hath he
provided this music?

ANTONIO

He is very busy about it. But, brother, I can tell you strange
news that you yet dreamt not of.

LEONATO

5   Are they good?

ANTONIO

As the events stamps them, but they have a good cover;
they show well outward. The Prince and Count Claudio,
walking in a thick-pleached alley in mine orchard, were
thus much overheard by a man of mine: the Prince
10   discovered to Claudio that he loved my niece your daughter
and meant to acknowledge it this night in a dance, and if he
found her accordant, he meant to take the present time by
the top and instantly break with you of it.

LEONATO

Hath the fellow any wit that told you this?

ANTONIO

15   A good sharp fellow. I will send for him, and question him
yourself.

ACT 1, SCENE 2

LEONATO *and* ANTONIO *enter.*

LEONATO

Hey, brother. Tell me, where is my nephew, your son? Has he taken care of the music?

ANTONIO

He is taking care of it as we speak. But brother, I have some strange news for you.

LEONATO

Is it good news?

ANTONIO

Well, it seems like good news. A servant of mine overheard the Prince and Claudio talking as they walked through my orchard. The Prince said that he is in love with Hero, your daughter, and that he is going to tell her so at the dance tonight. If he she wants to marry him, too, he's going to find you and ask for her hand immediately.

LEONATO

Is this servant of yours a smart man?

ANTONIO

He's very bright. I'll get him to come here, and you can ask him yourself.

LEONATO

No, no, we will hold it as a dream till it appear itself. But I
will acquaint my daughter withal, that she may be the
better prepared for an answer if peradventure this be true.
20   Go you and tell her of it.

Enter ANTONIO's *son, with a musician and attendants*

Cousins, you know what you have to do.—O, I cry you
mercy, friend. Go you with me and I will use your skill.—
Good cousin, have a care this busy time.

Exeunt

LEONATO

No, no, until it comes true we'll pretend it was just a dream we had. But my daughter should know about this, so she can be prepared with an answer just in case. Go to her and tell her for me.

ANTONIO's *son enters with a musician and attendants.*

Cousins, you all have work to do.—Oh, I beg your pardon. Come with me now, and help me out. —Dear cousin, please be careful during this busy time.

They all exit.

ACT 1, SCENE 3

Enter DON JOHN *and* CONRAD

CONRAD
What the goodyear, my lord, why are you thus out of
measure sad?

DON JOHN
There is no measure in the occasion that breeds. Therefore
the sadness is without limit.

CONRAD
5   You should hear reason.

DON JOHN
And when I have heard it, what blessing brings it?

CONRAD
If not a present remedy, at least a patient sufferance.

DON JOHN
I wonder that thou, being, as thou sayst thou art, born
under Saturn, goest about to apply a moral medicine to a
10   mortifying mischief. I cannot hide what I am. I must be sad
when I have cause and smile at no man's jests, eat when I
have stomach and wait for no man's leisure, sleep when I am
drowsy and tend on no man's business, laugh when I am
merry and claw no man in his humor.

CONRAD
15   Yea, but you must not make the full show of this till you
may do it without controlment. You have of late stood out
against your brother, and he hath ta'en you newly into his
grace, where it is impossible you should take true root but
by the fair weather that you make yourself. It is needful that
20   you frame the season for your own harvest.

ACT 1, SCENE 3

DON JOHN *and* CONRAD *enter.*

CONRAD

Really, my lord, why are you so excessively sad?

DON JOHN

The things that cause my sadness are without limit. Therefore my sadness is without limit.

CONRAD

You should listen to reason. Then you'd stop being so gloomy.

DON JOHN

And after I have sat and listened to reason, what's my prize?

CONRAD

If not an end to your suffering, then at least you'll have the means to endure it patiently.

DON JOHN

I'm amazed that you—being such a moody man yourself—are moralizing about my deadly condition. I can't hide what I am. I'll be sad when I have reason to be sad and won't smile at anybody's jokes. I'll eat when I'm hungry and won't wait until it's convenient. I'll sleep when I'm tired and won't rouse myself for anything. I'll laugh when I'm happy and won't flatter and fawn over anyone.

CONRAD

Sure, but don't do it at full volume until there's no danger in it. Not long ago you challenged and opposed your brother, and it is only very recently that he has forgiven you. You need to act carefully if you're going to stay in his good graces. You have to wait for the appropriate time to let loose.

DON JOHN
I had rather be a canker in a hedge than a rose in his grace,
and it better fits my blood to be disdained of all than to
fashion a carriage to rob love from any. In this, though I
cannot be said to be a flattering honest man, it must not be
25   denied but I am a plain-dealing villain. I am trusted with a
muzzle and enfranchised with a clog; therefore I have
decreed not to sing in my cage. If I had my mouth, I would
bite; if I had my liberty, I would do my liking. In the
meantime, let me be that I am, and seek not to alter me.

CONRAD
30   Can you make no use of your discontent?

DON JOHN
I make all use of it, for I use it only. Who comes here?

Enter BORACHIO

What news, Borachio?

BORACHIO
I came yonder from a great supper. The Prince your brother
is royally entertained by Leonato, and I can give you
35   intelligence of an intended marriage.

DON JOHN
Will it serve for any model to build mischief on? What is he
for a fool that betroths himself to unquietness?

BORACHIO
Marry, it is your brother's right hand.

DON JOHN
Who? The most exquisite Claudio?

BORACHIO
40   Even he.

DON JOHN

I'd rather be a weed in a hedge than a rose in my brother's garden. It suits me more to be hated by everyone than to put on a fancy show and trick people into loving me. Though I am not a flattering, righteous man, at least you can say that I am honest about being a villain. My brother trusts me now? Yeah—as much as a master trusts the dog he muzzles or the peasant he "frees" by chaining a big block around the man's foot. If my mouth were unrestrained, I'd bite. If I were free, I'd do what I pleased. Until that happens, let me be who I am and don't try to change me.

CONRAD

Can't you somehow use your dissatisfaction to your own advantage?

DON JOHN

I use it all the time, since it's all that I have. Who's that?

BORACHIO *enters.*

What's going on, Borachio?

BORACHIO

I just came from a great feast where Leonato is entertaining the Prince, your brother. I can give you information about an intended marriage.

DON JOHN

Will this give me an opportunity to make some mischief? Who is this fool who wants all the fuss of marriage?

BORACHIO

Your brother's right-hand man.

DON JOHN

Who? That pretty boy, Claudio?

BORACHIO

That's the one.

DON JOHN
> A proper squire. And who, and who? Which way looks he?

BORACHIO
> Marry, on Hero, the daughter and heir of Leonato.

DON JOHN
> A very forward March-chick! How came you to this?

BORACHIO
> Being entertained for a perfumer, as I was smoking a musty
> room, comes me the Prince and Claudio, hand in hand, in
> sad conference. I whipped me behind the arras, and there
> heard it agreed upon that the Prince should woo Hero for
> himself, and having obtained her, give her to Count
> Claudio.

DON JOHN
> Come, come, let us thither. This may prove food to my
> displeasure. That young start-up hath all the glory of my
> overthrow. If I can cross him any way, I bless myself every
> way. You are both sure, and will assist me?

CONRAD
> To the death, my lord.

DON JOHN
> Let us to the great supper. Their cheer is the greater that I
> am subdued. Would the cook were o' my mind! Shall we go
> prove what's to be done?

BORACHIO
> We'll wait upon your lordship.

Exeunt

DON JOHN

He's a very fancy gentleman. And who's the girl who has caught his eye?

BORACHIO

Hero, the daughter and heir of Leonato.

DON JOHN

A lively young one! How did you learn about this?

BORACHIO

I was hired to perfume all the rooms in Leonato's house. As I was working on one musty room, the Prince and Claudio entered. They were in the middle of a serious conversation. I quickly hid behind a tapestry and heard them agree that the Prince would court Hero tonight at the dance and, once he won her consent to marry, would give her to Claudio.

DON JOHN

Come, let's go to the dance. This just may cheer me up. Claudio, the young upstart, was responsible for keeping me from gaining power over my brother. If there's any way I can spoil his life, I'll be overjoyed. You'll both help me, right?

CONRAD

Until the day we die, my lord.

DON JOHN

Let's go to this great feast. They'll be even happier now that my mood has lightened. It's too bad the cook doesn't think like me; she would have poisoned them all if she did. Should we go check out the scene?

BORACHIO

Lead the way, sir.

They all exit.

ACT TWO

SCENE 1

Enter LEONATO, ANTONIO, HERO, BEATRICE, URSULA *and* MARGARET

LEONATO
Was not Count John here at supper?

ANTONIO
I saw him not.

BEATRICE
How tartly that gentleman looks! I never can see him but I am heartburned an hour after.

HERO
5   He is of a very melancholy disposition.

BEATRICE
He were an excellent man that were made just in the midway between him and Benedick. The one is too like an image and says nothing, and the other too like my lady's eldest son, evermore tattling.

LEONATO
10   Then half Signor Benedick's tongue in Count John's mouth, and half Count John's melancholy in Signor Benedick's face—

BEATRICE
With a good leg and a good foot, uncle, and money enough in his purse, such a man would win any woman in the
15   world, if he could get her goodwill.

LEONATO
By my troth, niece, thou wilt never get thee a husband if thou be so shrewd of thy tongue.

ANTONIO
In faith, she's too curst.

ACT TWO

SCENE 1

LEONATO, ANTONIO, HERO, BEATRICE, URSULA, *and*
MARGARET *enter.*

LEONATO

Wasn't Don John at dinner tonight?

ANTONIO

I didn't see him.

BEATRICE

That man always looks so sour! Just looking at him
gives me heartburn.

HERO

He has a very gloomy attitude.

BEATRICE

It would be excellent if they could make a man half-
way between Don John and Benedick. One of them is
too much like a painting of a man—he never speaks—
and the other is too much like a spoiled little boy,
always chattering.

LEONATO

So, the man would talk half as much as Benedick and
be half as serious as Don John—

BEATRICE

And if he were handsome, agile, and rich, too, he
could have any woman in the world—all he'd need
was her good will.

LEONATO

Really, niece, you'll never get a husband if you keep
saying such harsh things about people.

ANTONIO

Honestly, she is too ill-tempered.

BEATRICE
Too curst is more than curst. I shall lessen God's sending
20   that way, for it is said, "God sends a curst cow short horns,"
but to a cow too curst, he sends none.

LEONATO
So, by being too curst, God will send you no horns.

BEATRICE
Just, if he send me no husband, for the which blessing I am
at him upon my knees every morning and evening. Lord, I
25   could not endure a husband with a beard on his face! I had
rather lie in the woolen.

LEONATO
You may light on a husband that hath no beard.

BEATRICE
What should I do with him? Dress him in my apparel and
make him my waiting gentlewoman? He that hath a beard
30   is more than a youth, and he that hath no beard is less than
a man; and he that is more than a youth is not for me, and
he that is less than a man, I am not for him. Therefore I will
even take sixpence in earnest of the bearherd, and lead his
apes into hell.

LEONATO
35   Well then, go you into hell?

BEATRICE
No, but to the gate, and there will the devil meet me like an
old cuckold with horns on his head, and say, "Get you to
heaven, Beatrice, get you to heaven; here's no place for you
maids." So deliver I up my apes and away to Saint Peter. For
40   the heavens, he shows me where the bachelors sit, and there
live we as merry as the day is long.

BEATRICE

Being "too ill-tempered" is different from being simply "ill-tempered," right? So I suppose that means I can escape God's punishment, for in the old proverb, it is said that "God gives an ill-tempered cow short horns" so that she can't inflict damage on anyone. But it doesn't say anything about a cow that is *too* ill-tempered.

LEONATO

So then, for being too argumentative, God won't send you any horns?

BEATRICE

By saying God won't give her horns, Beatrice jokes that she won't have a husband.

Exactly. I pray every morning and night that the Lord won't send me a husband. Really, I couldn't stand a husband with a beard. I'd rather be wrapped in scratchy blankets all night.

LEONATO

Maybe you will find a husband without a beard.

BEATRICE

And then what would I do with him? Dress him up in my clothes and pretend he's my lady servant? If he has a beard, he's more than a boy; if he doesn't have a beard, he's less than a man. If he's more than a boy, he's not the one for me, and if he's less than a man, I'm not the one for him. They say that women who die unmarried are destined to lead the apes to hell, and I suppose that'll be my fate as well.

LEONATO

So you'll go to hell?

BEATRICE

No, just to the gates of hell, where the devil will meet me, with the horns on his head like a cuckold, and say, "Go up to heaven, Beatrice. Hell is no place for you virgins." So I'll fly up to heaven (leaving the apes behind) where I'll be met by Saint Peter guarding heaven's gates. He will show me the part of heaven where the bachelors sit, and I'll have fun there forever.

ANTONIO

    (to HERO*)* Well, niece, I trust you will be ruled by your
    father.

BEATRICE

    Yes, faith, it is my cousin's duty to make curtsy and say,
45   "Father, as it please you." But yet for all that, cousin, let
    him be a handsome fellow, or else make another curtsy and
    say, "Father, as it please me."

LEONATO

    Well, niece, I hope to see you one day fitted with a husband.

BEATRICE

    Not till God make men of some other metal than earth.
50   Would it not grieve a woman to be overmastered with a
    piece of valiant dust? To make an account of her life to a clod
    of wayward marl? No, uncle, I'll none. Adam's sons are my
    brethren, and truly I hold it a sin to match in my kindred.

LEONATO

    (to HERO*)* Daughter, remember what I told you. If the
55   Prince do solicit you in that kind, you know your answer.

BEATRICE

    The fault will be in the music, cousin, if you be not wooed
    in good time. If the Prince be too important, tell him there
    is measure in everything, and so dance out the answer. For
    hear me, Hero, wooing, wedding, and repenting is as a
60   Scotch jig, a measure, and a cinquepace. The first suit is hot
    and hasty like a Scotch jig, and full as fantastical; the
    wedding, mannerly modest as a measure, full of state and
    ancientry; and then comes repentance, and with his bad
    legs falls into the cinquepace faster and faster till he sink
65   into his grave.

ANTONIO

(to HERO) Well, niece, I trust that you will defer to your father on these important decisions.

BEATRICE

Surely, my cousin has a duty to please her father. But if the husband her father chooses isn't handsome, she should sweetly tell her father that she will please herself—with another one.

LEONATO

Well, niece, I hope that I will see you married one day.

BEATRICE

No, I won't take a husband until they make men out of something other than dirt. What woman wouldn't be distressed, being lorded over by a handful of dust? Can you imagine being hitched to a lump of clay? No, uncle, I won't be married. And anyhow, if Adam is the father of all mankind, then his sons are my brothers, and really I believe that incest is a sin.

Adam, the biblical father of mankind, is said to be made from "the dust of the ground" (Genesis 2:7).

LEONATO

(to HERO) Daughter, remember what I told you. If the Prince asks for your hand in marriage, you know what to tell him.

BEATRICE

But cousin, make sure he woos you properly and appropriately. If he is too insistent, tell him that romance is like a dance: it has its own rhythm and timing. Look, the three stages of romance are like three different dances. The wooing is like a Scottish jig: hot and fast and full of whimsy and illusion. The wedding is a like a dance you would do before the King: proper and decorous. Finally, you get to the part where you regret having gotten married in the first place. It is like the lively cinquepace: it goes faster and faster until you eventually topple over and die.

Cinquepace is an energetic five-step dance.

LEONATO
> Cousin, you apprehend passing shrewdly.

BEATRICE
> I have a good eye, uncle. I can see a church by daylight.

LEONATO
> The revelers are entering, brother. Make good room.

> *Enter* DON PEDRO, CLAUDIO, BENEDICK, BALTHASAR, DON
> JOHN, BORACHIO, MARGARET, URSULA *and others*, *masked*

DON PEDRO
> Lady, will you walk a bout with your friend?

> *They begin to dance*

HERO
70   So you walk softly, and look sweetly, and say nothing, I am
> yours for the walk, and especially when I walk away.

DON PEDRO
> With me in your company?

HERO
> I may say so when I please.

DON PEDRO
> And when please you to say so?

HERO
75   When I like your favor, for God defend the lute should be
> like the case!

DON PEDRO
> My visor is Philemon's roof; within the house is Jove.

LEONATO

Niece, you are exceptionally perceptive.

BEATRICE

I have a good eye, uncle. I can see what's in broad daylight.

LEONATO

The partygoers have arrived. Let's give them room.

DON PEDRO, CLAUDIO, BENEDICK, BALTHASAR, DON JOHN, BORACHIO, MARGARET, URSULA enter along with other partygoers. They're all wearing masks.

DON PEDRO

My lady, will you have a dance with me?

They begin to dance.

HERO

As long as you move gracefully, look handsome, and say nothing, I'm yours for the dance. And I'll even linger after I've gone.

DON PEDRO

Will I be with you then?

HERO

Perhaps, if I decide to let you.

DON PEDRO

And when will that be?

HERO

When I like the way you look, for God forbid your face be as ugly as your mask!

DON PEDRO

Philemon was a peasant who entertained the disguised Jove in his humble cottage.

My mask is like the roof of the poor Philemon's humble cottage; underneath the mask, I am as magnificent as the glorious god Jove.

HERO
> Why, then, your visor should be thatched.

DON PEDRO
> Speak low if you speak love.

They move aside. BALTHASAR *and* MARGARET *move forward*

BALTHASAR
80 > Well, I would you did like me.

MARGARET
> So would not I for your own sake, for I have many ill qualities.

BALTHASAR
> Which is one?

MARGARET
> I say my prayers aloud.

BALTHASAR
> I love you the better; the hearers may cry "Amen."

MARGARET
85 > God match me with a good dancer!

BALTHASAR
> Amen.

MARGARET
> And God keep him out of my sight when the dance is done!
> Answer, clerk.

BALTHASAR
> No more words. The clerk is answered.

They move aside. URSULA *and* ANTONIO *move forward.*

URSULA
90 > I know you well enough. You are Signor Antonio.

ANTONIO
> At a word, I am not.

URSULA
> I know you by the waggling of your head.

HERO

Well, then, since Philemon's roof was thatched with straw, your mask should have a beard.

DON PEDRO

If you wish to speak of love, speak more softly.

They move aside. BALTHASAR *and* MARGARET *move forward.*

BALTHASAR

Well, I wish you liked me.

MARGARET

I'm glad I don't, for your sake. I have many awful qualities.

BALTHASAR

Tell me one.

MARGARET

I say my prayers out loud.

BALTHASAR

That makes me love you even more. Everyone who hears you can shout, "Amen."

MARGARET

God give me a good dance partner!

BALTHASAR

Amen. That would be me.

MARGARET

And God take him away from me when we're finished dancing! Go ahead—say "Amen."

BALTHASAR

No more talking. I've got my answer.

They move aside. URSULA *and* ANTONIO *move forward.*

URSULA

I know who you are; you are Signior Antonio.

ANTONIO

No, really, I'm not.

URSULA

I can tell by the way you waggle your head.

ANTONIO
> To tell you true, I counterfeit him.

URSULA
> You could never do him so ill-well unless you were the very
95   man. Here's his dry hand up and down. You are he, you are
> he.

ANTONIO
> At a word, I am not.

URSULA
> Come, come, do you think I do not know you by your
> excellent wit? Can virtue hide itself? Go to, mum, you are
100 he. Graces will appear, and there's an end.

> *They move aside.* **BENEDICK** *and* **BEATRICE** *move forward.*

BEATRICE
> Will you not tell me who told you so?

BENEDICK
> No, you shall pardon me.

BEATRICE
> Nor will you not tell me who you are?

BENEDICK
> Not now.

BEATRICE
105 That I was disdainful and that I had my good wit out of The
> Hundred Merry Tales! Well this was Signor Benedick that
> said so.

BENEDICK
> What's he?

BEATRICE
> I am sure you know him well enough.

BENEDICK
110 Not I, believe me.

BEATRICE
> Did he never make you laugh?

ANTONIO

Really, I'm only pretending to be him.

URSULA

You could only imitate his imperfections so well if you were the man himself. Look, you've got his wrinkled hands. You are Antonio, you are he.

ANTONIO

In short, I'm not.

URSULA

Come on, do you think I can't recognize you by your excellent wit? Can a good thing hide itself? Be quiet, you are Antonio. A man's virtues will always show themselves, and that's the end of that.

They move aside. BENEDICK *and* BEATRICE *move forward.*

BEATRICE

Won't you tell me who told you that?

BENEDICK

No, you'll have to excuse me.

BEATRICE

And you won't tell me who you are?

BENEDICK

Not now.

BEATRICE

Who said that I was disdainful, and that I got all my best lines out of a bad joke book?! Well, it must have been Signior Benedick.

BENEDICK

Who's that?

BEATRICE

I'm sure you know him.

BENEDICK

No I don't, believe me.

BEATRICE

What, he never made you laugh?

BENEDICK

I pray you, what is he?

BEATRICE

Why, he is the Prince's jester, a very dull fool, only his gift
is in devising impossible slanders. None but libertines
115   delight in him, and the commendation is not in his wit but
in his villainy, for he both pleases men and angers them,
and then they laugh at him and beat him. I am sure he is in
the fleet. I would he had boarded me.

BENEDICK

When I know the gentleman, I'll tell him what you say.

BEATRICE

120   Do, do. He'll but break a comparison or two on me, which,
peradventure not marked or not laughed at, strikes him into
melancholy, and then there's a partridge wing saved, for the
fool will eat no supper that night.

Music for the dance

We must follow the leaders.

BENEDICK

125   In every good thing.

BEATRICE

Nay, if they lead to any ill, I will leave them at the next
turning.

Dance, then exeunt all except
DON JOHN, BORACHIO, *and* CLAUDIO

DON JOHN

(to BORACHIO*)* Sure my brother is amorous on Hero, and
hath withdrawn her father to break with him about it. The
130   ladies follow her, and but one visor remains.

BENEDICK

Please tell me, who is this man?

BEATRICE

Why, he's the Prince's fool, and a very dull fool at that. His only talent is his capacity to come up with unbelievable slanders. Only the most immoral people enjoy his company, and they like him not for his wit but his outrageousness. He manages to both please and anger people; they laugh at him and then beat him up. I'm sure he's out there dancing. I could have sworn he trampled on me.

BENEDICK

When I meet this gentleman, I'll tell him what you've said.

BEATRICE

Oh, please do. He'll say a few nasty things about me, and if nobody listens to him or laughs, he'll be thrown into a funk. And that will save a partridge wing from being eaten, because he'll be too miserable for dinner.

Music for the dance begins.

Come on, we have to follow the leaders of the dance.

BENEDICK

In every good thing they do.

BEATRICE

No, if they try to lead us to harm, I will leave the dance floor at the next song.

There is a dance. Everyone exits except **DON JOHN**, **BORACHIO**, *and* **CLAUDIO**.

DON JOHN

(*to* **BORACHIO**) My brother just wooed Hero and now has taken her father inside to tell him his feelings. The ladies have followed Hero, but one masked man remains.

BORACHIO
And that is Claudio. I know him by his bearing.

DON JOHN
(to CLAUDIO) Are not you Signor Benedick?

CLAUDIO
You know me well. I am he.

DON JOHN
Signor, you are very near my brother in his love. He is
135   enamored on Hero. I pray you, dissuade him from her. She
is no equal for his birth. You may do the part of an honest
man in it.

CLAUDIO
How know you he loves her?

DON JOHN
I heard him swear his affection.

BORACHIO
140   So did I too, and he swore he would marry her tonight.

DON JOHN
Come, let us to the banquet.

Exeunt DON JOHN *and* BORACHIO

CLAUDIO
(unmasking)
Thus answer I in the name of Benedick,
But hear these ill news with the ears of Claudio.
'Tis certain so, the Prince woos for himself.
145   Friendship is constant in all other things
Save in the office and affairs of love.
Therefore all hearts in love use their own tongues.
Let every eye negotiate for itself
And trust no agent, for beauty is a witch
150   Against whose charms faith melteth into blood.
This is an accident of hourly proof,
Which I mistrusted not. Farewell, therefore, Hero.

Enter BENEDICK

BORACHIO

That's Claudio. I can tell by the way he carries himself.

DON JOHN

(to CLAUDIO*)* Aren't you Signior Benedick?

CLAUDIO

You know me too well. I am Benedick.

DON JOHN

Sir, my brother is very fond of you. He is in love with Hero. Please make him change his mind. She doesn't have the proper rank to marry the Prince. You would be doing a good service.

CLAUDIO

How do you know he loves her?

DON JOHN

I heard him swear he did.

BORACHIO

I did too, and he also swore he would marry her tonight.

DON JOHN

Come on, let's get to the banquet.

DON JOHN *and* BORACHIO *exit.*

CLAUDIO

(taking off his mask)

Though I said my name was Benedick, I heard this news with Claudio's ears. Of course the Prince wants Hero for himself. Friendship is enduring except when love is involved. Therefore, all lovers should speak for themselves. They should look for themselves, without asking someone else to get involved in their affairs. Beauty is a witch whose spells can turn loyalty into passion. This happens a lot, but it didn't occur to me that it would happen to me. Goodbye then, Hero.

BENEDICK *enters.*

BENEDICK
Count Claudio?

CLAUDIO
Yea, the same.

BENEDICK
155   Come, will you go with me?

CLAUDIO
Whither?

BENEDICK
Even to the next willow, about your own business, county.
What fashion will you wear the garland of? About your
neck like an usurer's chain? Or under your arm like a
160   lieutenant's scarf? You must wear it one way, for the Prince
hath got your Hero.

CLAUDIO
I wish him joy of her.

BENEDICK
Why, that's spoken like an honest drover; so they sell
bullocks. But did you think the Prince would have served
165   you thus?

CLAUDIO
I pray you, leave me.

BENEDICK
Ho, now you strike like the blind man. 'Twas the boy that
stole your meat, and you'll beat the post.

CLAUDIO
If it will not be, I'll leave you.

Exit

BENEDICK

Claudio?

CLAUDIO

Yes, that's me.

BENEDICK

Will you come with me?

CLAUDIO

Where?

BENEDICK

The willow tree is a symbol of unrequited love.

Right over to that willow tree to see about your business. How do you want to wear your garland of willow leaves? Around your neck, like a moneylender's gold chain, or under your arm, like a lieutenant's sash? You have to wear it somehow, because the Prince has gotten your Hero.

CLAUDIO

I hope he enjoys her.

BENEDICK

You sound like a cattle dealer: that's the way they sell bulls. But do you really think the Prince would treat you that way?

CLAUDIO

Please, leave me alone.

BENEDICK

Look at you, thrashing about like a blind man. A boy robbed you, but you'll beat up the post instead.

CLAUDIO

If you won't leave, then *I'll* leave.

He exits.

BENEDICK

170   Alas, poor hurt fowl, now will he creep into sedges. But that
my Lady Beatrice should know me, and not know me! The
Prince's fool! Ha, it may be I go under that title because I am
merry. Yea, but so I am apt to do myself wrong. I am not so
reputed! It is the base, though bitter, disposition of Beatrice
175   that puts the world into her person and so gives me out.
Well, I'll be revenged as I may.

Enter DON PEDRO

DON PEDRO

Now, Signior, where's the Count? Did you see him?

BENEDICK

Troth, my lord, I have played the part of Lady Fame. I
found him here as melancholy as a lodge in a warren. I told
180   him, and I think I told him true, that your Grace had got the
goodwill of this young lady, and I offered him my company
to a willow tree, either to make him a garland, as being
forsaken, or to bind him up a rod, as being worthy to be
whipped.

DON PEDRO

185   To be whipped? What's his fault?

BENEDICK

The flat transgression of a schoolboy who, being overjoyed
with finding a birds' nest, shows it his companion, and he
steals it.

DON PEDRO

Wilt thou make a trust a transgression? The transgression
190   is in the stealer.

BENEDICK

Oh, the poor bird. Now he'll hide himself in the bushes. But how strange that Beatrice should seem to know who I was and yet not know at the same time. "The Prince's fool"! Maybe they call me that because I am cheerful. Yes, but I am insulting myself by thinking this way. I don't have that kind of reputation! Beatrice's mean, sarcastic nature makes her believe that the entire world shares her opinions; that's why she describes me this way. Well, I'll get my revenge.

DON PEDRO *enters.*

DON PEDRO

Now, sir, where is Claudio? Did you see him?

BENEDICK

Yes, my lord, I played the part of a gossip and brought him the news. I found him here, as sad as a rabbit in a burrow. I told him—and I think I was telling the truth—that you had won the lady's heart. I offered to accompany him to the willow tree, where he could either make a garland—fit to be worn by an abandoned lover—or gather sticks into a bundle, ready for his beating.

Many disagree about what the original line means. Another translation may be: "as sad as a solitary house in an open field."

DON PEDRO

Beating? Why, what did he do?

BENEDICK

He was like a schoolboy who finds a bird's nest and happily shows it to his friend, who then steals it from him.

DON PEDRO

What, is trusting a friend such a crime? The criminal is the one who stole the nest.

BENEDICK

Yet it had not been amiss the rod had been made, and the
garland too, for the garland he might have worn himself
and the rod he might have bestowed on you, who, as I take
it, have stolen his birds' nest.

DON PEDRO

195   I will but teach them to sing and restore them to the owner.

BENEDICK

If their singing answer your saying, by my faith, you say
honestly.

DON PEDRO

The Lady Beatrice hath a quarrel to you. The gentleman
that danced with her told her she is much wronged by you.

BENEDICK

200   O, she misused me past the endurance of a block! An oak
but with one green leaf on it would have answered her. My
very visor began to assume life and scold with her. She told
me, not thinking I had been myself, that I was the Prince's
jester, that I was duller than a great thaw, huddling jest
205   upon jest with such impossible conveyance upon me that I
stood like a man at a mark with a whole army shooting at
me. She speaks poniards, and every word stabs. If her
breath were as terrible as her terminations, there were no
living near her; she would infect to the north star. I would
210   not marry her, though she were endowed with all that
Adam had left him before he transgressed. She would have
made Hercules have turned spit, yea, and have cleft his club
to make the fire, too. Come, talk not of her. You shall find
her the infernal Ate in good apparel. I would to God some
215   scholar would conjure her, for certainly, while she is here,
a man may live as quiet in hell as in a sanctuary, and people
sin upon purpose because they would go thither. So indeed
all disquiet, horror and perturbation follows her.

BENEDICK

It might have been appropriate to make both the rod and the garland. He could have worn the garland himself and beaten you with the rod, since you—as I understand it—have stolen his bird's nest.

DON PEDRO

I only want to teach the baby birds to sing; then I will return the nest to its rightful owner.

BENEDICK

We'll wait and see; if the chicks follow your lead—if Hero is ready to love Claudio—then we'll know you're telling the truth.

DON PEDRO

Lady Beatrice is angry with you. The gentleman she danced with told her you insulted her.

BENEDICK

Not even a block of wood could handle her abuses! An oak tree barely clinging to life would have revived itself to fight her. Even my mask seemed to come to life in order to argue with her. She told me—not realizing it was me—that I was the Prince's jester and as dull as mud. She hurled mocking insults at me with such incredible speed that all I could do was stand there, paralyzed. She speaks daggers, and every word stabs. If her breath were as terrible as her words, she would kill every living thing from here to the furthest star. I wouldn't marry her, even if she were as blessed as paradise. If she were married to the great hero Hercules, she would have humiliated him with chores around the house and ordered him to chop up his famous club for firewood. Please, don't mention her. She's as wicked as Ate, just disguised in pretty clothes. I wish to God that some wise man would conjure her away, because as long as she lives on earth, our lives are filled with turmoil. It's quieter in hell, where people, sinning on purpose, are eager to be sent just to get away from her. So chaos, horror, and sorrow follow her wherever she goes.

Ate was the goddess of conflict.

Enter CLAUDIO, BEATRICE, HERO, *and* LEONATO

DON PEDRO
Look, here she comes.

BENEDICK
220   Will your grace command me any service to the world's
end? I will go on the slightest errand now to the Antipodes
that you can devise to send me on. I will fetch you a
toothpicker now from the furthest inch of Asia, bring you
the length of Prester John's foot, fetch you a hair off the
225   great Cham's beard, do you any embassage to the Pygmies,
rather than hold three words' conference with this harpy.
You have no employment for me?

DON PEDRO
None but to desire your good company.

BENEDICK
O God, sir, here's a dish I love not. I cannot endure my
230   Lady Tongue!

Exit

DON PEDRO
(to BEATRICE*)* Come, lady, come, you have lost the heart of
Signior Benedick.

BEATRICE
Indeed, my lord, he lent it me awhile, and I gave him use for
it, a double heart for his single one. Marry, once before he
235   won it of me with false dice. Therefore your Grace may well
say I have lost it.

DON PEDRO
You have put him down, lady, you have put him down.

CLAUDIO, BEATRICE, HERO, *and* LEONATO *enter.*

DON PEDRO

Look, here she comes.

BENEDICK

Your highness, could you send me on a mission to the ends of the earth? I'll go to the Antipodes for any little errand you can think of. I'll fetch you a toothpick from the farthest reaches of Asia, or find out Prester John's shoe size, or snatch a hair from Kublai Khan's beard, or deliver any message you wish to relay to the Pygmies—anything rather than exchange three words with this awful, screeching woman. Isn't there something you want from me?

Fantastical items located in distant lands.

DON PEDRO

Nothing but your good company.

BENEDICK

Oh, God, sir, here comes a dish I hate. I can't stand tongue.

He exits.

DON PEDRO

(to BEATRICE*)* Lady, you have lost Signior Benedick's heart.

BEATRICE

It's true, my lord. He lent it to me once, and I paid him back with interest: a double heart for his single one. Really, he won it from me once before in a dishonest game of dice. So I suppose your grace can truly say that I have lost it.

DON PEDRO

You've humiliated him, lady: you've put him down.

BEATRICE
So I would not he should do me, my lord, lest I should prove
the mother of fools. I have brought Count Claudio, whom
240   you sent me to seek.

DON PEDRO
Why, how now, Count, wherefore are you sad?

CLAUDIO
Not sad, my lord.

DON PEDRO
How then, sick?

CLAUDIO
Neither, my lord.

BEATRICE
245   The Count is neither sad, nor sick, nor merry, nor well, but
civil count, civil as an orange, and something of that jealous
complexion.

DON PEDRO
I' faith, lady, I think your blazon to be true, though, I'll be
sworn, if he be so, his conceit is false.—Here, Claudio, I
250   have wooed in thy name, and fair Hero is won. I have broke
with her father and his goodwill obtained. Name the day of
marriage, and God give thee joy.

LEONATO
Count, take of me my daughter, and with her my fortunes.
His grace hath made the match, and all grace say "Amen"
255   to it.

BEATRICE
Speak, Count, 'tis your cue.

CLAUDIO
Silence is the perfectest herald of joy. I were but little happy
if I could say how much.—Lady, as you are mine, I am
yours. I give away myself for you and dote upon the
260   exchange.

BEATRICE

Beatrice means "put down" in the sense of to "take to bed."

And I hope that he won't put *me* down or I'm sure to have fools for children. I've brought Claudio, who you sent me to find.

DON PEDRO

Why, what's wrong, count? Why are you so sad?

CLAUDIO

I'm not sad, my lord.

DON PEDRO

What then, sick?

CLAUDIO

I'm neither, my lord.

BEATRICE

Beatrice puns with the name of a town in Spain famous for its oranges.

The count is neither sad nor sick nor cheerful nor well—he's just civil, as Seville as an orange, with the same jealous-yellow complexion.

DON PEDRO

Truly, lady, I think your description is correct, though I swear he has no reason to look like that. Here, Claudio, I've wooed Hero for you, and she's agreed to marry you. I've told her father, and he's given his permission. Tell us when you wish to get married, and may God give you joy.

LEONATO

Claudio, take my daughter, and, with her, take my fortunes. The Prince has made the match, and may God bless it.

BEATRICE

Speak, Claudio, that's your cue.

CLAUDIO

Complete joy makes one speechless; if I were only a little happy, then I could say exactly how much. Lady, you are mine and I am yours. For you, I give myself away and I'm ecstatic about the exchange.

BEATRICE
Speak, cousin, or if you cannot, stop his mouth with a kiss
and let not him speak neither.

DON PEDRO
In faith, lady, you have a merry heart.

BEATRICE
Yea, my lord. I thank it, poor fool, it keeps on the windy side
265   of care. My cousin tells him in his ear that he is in her heart.

CLAUDIO
And so she doth, cousin.

BEATRICE
Good Lord for alliance! Thus goes everyone to the world
but I, and I am sunburnt. I may sit in a corner and cry,
"Heigh-ho for a husband!"

DON PEDRO
270   Lady Beatrice, I will get you one.

BEATRICE
I would rather have one of your father's getting. Hath your
grace ne'er a brother like you? Your father got excellent
husbands, if a maid could come by them.

DON PEDRO
Will you have me, lady?

BEATRICE
275   No, my lord, unless I might have another for working days.
Your Grace is too costly to wear every day. But I beseech
your Grace pardon me. I was born to speak all mirth and no
matter.

DON PEDRO
Your silence most offends me, and to be merry best
280   becomes you, for out o' question you were born in a merry
hour.

BEATRICE

> Say something, cousin. Or, if you can't say anything, stop his mouth with a kiss and don't let him speak, either.

DON PEDRO

> Truly, lady, you have a merry heart.

BEATRICE

> Yes, my lord. I thank my heart—the poor fool—for it keeps away from seriousness. Look, my cousin is whispering to Claudio that she loves him.

CLAUDIO

> Why, you're absolutely right, cousin.

BEATRICE

> Thank the lord for alliances! So everyone goes off into the world except me, who stays in because I'm sunburned. I should sit in the corner and sing that song, "Heigh-Ho for a Husband!"

DON PEDRO

> Lady Beatrice, I'll get you a husband.

BEATRICE

> I'd rather get a husband from your father. Don't you have any brothers like you? Your father's sons would make excellent husbands, if only a girl could catch one for herself.

DON PEDRO

> Will you take me, my lady?

BEATRICE

> No, my lord, unless I could have another husband for the work week. You are too expensive to wear every day. But please, forgive me, your highness. I was born to speak cleverly, not seriously.

DON PEDRO

> I'd be more offended if you were silent, for being lively and cheerful suits you best. Surely, you must have been born at a happy time.

BEATRICE
No, sure, my lord, my mother cried, but then there was a star danced, and under that was I born.—Cousins, God give you joy!

LEONATO
285   Niece, will you look to those things I told you of?

BEATRICE
I cry you mercy, uncle.—By your Grace's pardon.

Exit

DON PEDRO
By my troth, a pleasant-spirited lady.

LEONATO
There's little of the melancholy element in her, my lord. She is never sad but when she sleeps, and not ever sad then, for
290   I have heard my daughter say she hath often dreamed of unhappiness and waked herself with laughing.

DON PEDRO
She cannot endure to hear tell of a husband.

LEONATO
Oh, by no means. She mocks all her wooers out of suit.

DON PEDRO
She were an excellent wife for Benedict.

LEONATO
295   O Lord, my lord, if they were but a week married, they would talk themselves mad.

DON PEDRO
County Claudio, when mean you to go to church?

CLAUDIO
Tomorrow, my lord. Time goes on crutches till love have all his rites.

BEATRICE

Actually, my lord, my mother cried when she was giving birth to me. But then a star danced in the sky, and that's the moment I was born.—Kinsmen, I'm off.

LEONATO

Niece, will you take care of those things I mentioned?

BEATRICE

Oh, yes, I'm sorry, uncle.—If you'll excuse me, your grace.

She exits.

DON PEDRO

I swear, she's a very good-natured lady.

LEONATO

There's very little about her that's gloomy, my lord. She's only sad when she sleeps—and not even then. Hero told me that Beatrice has often had dreams about being unhappy, and managed to wake herself from them by laughing.

DON PEDRO

She can't stand to hear about getting a husband.

LEONATO

No, not at all. She mocks all her suitors so severely that they drop the suit.

DON PEDRO

She would make a good wife for Benedick.

LEONATO

Oh, Lord, if they were married, they'd drive themselves crazy within a week.

DON PEDRO

Count Claudio, when do you plan to go to church and be married?

CLAUDIO

Tomorrow, my lord. Time will move as slowly as an old man until our love receives its proper ceremony.

LEONATO

300   Not till Monday, my dear son, which is hence a just
        sevennight, and a time too brief, too, to have all things
        answer my mind.

DON PEDRO

        (to CLAUDIO*)* Come, you shake the head at so long a
        breathing, but I warrant thee, Claudio, the time shall not go
305   dully by us. I will in the interim undertake one of Hercules'
        labors, which is to bring Signor Benedick and the Lady
        Beatrice into a mountain of affection, th' one with th' other.
        I would fain have it a match, and I doubt not but to fashion
        it, if you three will but minister such assistance as I shall
310   give you direction.

LEONATO

        My lord, I am for you, though it cost me ten nights'
        watchings.

CLAUDIO

        And I, my lord.

DON PEDRO

        And you too, gentle Hero?

HERO

315   I will do any modest office, my lord, to help my cousin to a
        good husband.

DON PEDRO

        And Benedick is not the unhopefulest husband that I know.
        Thus far can I praise him: he is of a noble strain, of approved
        valor, and confirmed honesty. I will teach you how to humor
320   your cousin that she shall fall in love with Benedick.—And
        I, with your two helps, will so practice on Benedick
        that, in despite of his quick wit and his queasy stomach, he
        shall fall in love with Beatrice. If we can do this, Cupid is no
        longer an archer; his glory shall be ours, for we are the only
325   love gods. Go in with me, and I will tell you my drift.

                                                        Exeunt

LEONATO

Wait till Monday, my dear son, which is only a week away. Even that is too short a time to plan things the way I would like.

DON PEDRO

(to CLAUDIO) Oh, don't look so frustrated at having to wait so long. I promise you, Claudio, the time will go by quickly. While we're waiting for the wedding, I'm going to take on an impossible task: to make Signior Benedick and the Lady Beatrice fall in love with each other. I aim to see them matched, and with all of your help, I'm sure we can make it happen.

LEONATO

My lord, I will help you, even if it means I have to stay awake for ten nights straight.

CLAUDIO

Me too, my lord.

DON PEDRO

And you, sweet Hero?

HERO

I'll do any decent thing, my lord, to help my cousin get a good husband.

DON PEDRO

And Benedick is not the worst husband I can think of. This much I can say about him: he is well-born, has proven his bravery in battle, and has established his good character. Hero, I'll show you how to influence your cousin so she falls in love with Benedick. We men will trick Benedick so that, despite his quick wit and his queasiness about marriage, he will fall in love with her. If we can do this, then we will steal Cupid's glory. We will be the supreme love gods! Come inside with me, and I will tell you my plan.

They all exit.

ACT 2, SCENE 2

Enter DON JOHN *and* BORACHIO

DON JOHN

It is so. The Count Claudio shall marry the daughter of
Leonato.

BORACHIO

Yea, my lord, but I can cross it.

DON JOHN

Any bar, any cross, any impediment will be med'cinable to
5   me. I am sick in displeasure to him, and whatsoever comes
athwart his affection ranges evenly with mine. How canst
thou cross this marriage?

BORACHIO

Not honestly, my lord, but so covertly that no dishonesty
shall appear in me.

DON JOHN

10   Show me briefly how.

BORACHIO

I think I told your lordship a year since how much I am in
the favor of Margaret, the waiting gentlewoman to Hero.

DON JOHN

I remember.

BORACHIO

I can, at any unseasonable instant of the night, appoint her
15   to look out at her lady's chamber window.

DON JOHN

What life is in that to be the death of this marriage?

BORACHIO

The poison of that lies in you to temper. Go you to the
Prince your brother. Spare not to tell him that he hath
wronged his honor in marrying the renowned Claudio,
20   whose estimation do you mightily hold up, to a
contaminated stale, such a one as Hero.

ACT 2, SCENE 2

Enter DON JOHN *and* BORACHIO

DON JOHN

It's arranged. The Count Claudio will marry Leonato's daughter.

BORACHIO

Yes, my lord, but I can spoil it.

DON JOHN

Any obstacle or barrier to Claudio's happiness will be like medicine to me. I hate him so much it makes me sick, and whoever can ruin his happiness will make me happy. How will you wreck this marriage?

BORACHIO

I can only do it by lying, my lord, but I can do it so secretly that no one will suspect me.

DON JOHN

Quickly, tell me how.

BORACHIO

I think it was a year ago that I told you how much Margaret, Hero's servant woman, likes me.

DON JOHN

I remember.

BORACHIO

I can arrange it so that at some indecent hour of the night, she looks out Hero's bedroom window.

DON JOHN

How will that kill this marriage?

BORACHIO

That part is up to you. Go to the Prince, your brother, and tell him that he has done a terrible thing by matching the renowned Claudio—whom you greatly admire—with such a tainted whore as Hero.

DON JOHN

What proof shall I make of that?

BORACHIO

Proof enough to misuse the Prince, to vex Claudio, to undo
Hero, and kill Leonato. Look you for any other issue?

DON JOHN

25   Only to despite them, I will endeavor anything.

BORACHIO

Go then, find me a meet hour to draw Don Pedro and the
Count Claudio alone. Tell them that you know that Hero
loves me. Intend a kind of zeal both to the Prince and
Claudio, as in love of your brother's honor, who hath made
30   this match, and his friend's reputation, who is thus like to
be cozened with the semblance of a maid, that you have
discovered thus. They will scarcely believe this without
trial. Offer them instances, which shall bear no less
likelihood than to see me at her chamber window, hear me
35   call Margaret "Hero," hear Margaret term me "Claudio,"
and bring them to see this the very night before the
intended wedding, for in the meantime I will so fashion the
matter that Hero shall be absent, and there shall appear
such seeming truth of Hero's disloyalty that jealousy shall
40   be called assurance and all the preparation overthrown.

DON JOHN

Grow this to what adverse issue it can, I will put it in
practice. Be cunning in the working this, and thy fee is a
thousand ducats.

BORACHIO

Be you constant in the accusation, and my cunning shall not
45   shame me.

DON JOHN

I will presently go learn their day of marriage.

Exeunt

DON JOHN

What will be my evidence?

BORACHIO

Evidence enough to deceive the Prince, anger Claudio, ruin Hero, and kill Leonato. Is there anything else you wish?

DON JOHN

That's all I want, and I'll do anything to accomplish it.

BORACHIO

Find a time to speak with Don Pedro and Claudio alone. Tell them you know that Hero loves me. Pretend to be very concerned about both the Prince, who has compromised his honor by making the match, and Claudio, whose reputation will be ruined by this woman who's pretending to be a virgin. Of course, they won't believe you without proof. Tell them you've seen the two of us at Hero's bedroom window, and then bring them to see for themselves on the night before the wedding. I'll arrange it so that Hero is away for the night, so what they'll actually see is Margaret and me at the window, calling each other "Hero" and "Claudio." It'll be such blatant evidence of Hero's disloyalty that Claudio's jealousy will quickly turn to certainty, and the wedding will be instantly called off.

Some editors assume "Claudio" is an error, and change it to "Borachio." ⟶

DON JOHN

Make the arrangements, and I'll do it. Do this carefully, and I will reward you with a thousand gold coins.

BORACHIO

If you make the accusation convincingly, then my cunning won't fail me.

DON JOHN

I'll go now to find out the date of the wedding.

They exit.

ACT 2, SCENE 3

Enter BENEDICK

BENEDICK
Boy!

Enter BOY

BOY
Signior?

BENEDICK
In my chamber window lies a book. Bring it hither to me in the orchard.

BOY
5   I am here already, sir.

BENEDICK
I know that, but I would have thee hence and here again.

Exit BOY

I do much wonder that one man, seeing how much another man is a fool when he dedicates his behaviors to love, will, after he hath laughed at such shallow follies in others,
10   become the argument of his own scorn by falling in love—and such a man is Claudio. I have known when there was no music with him but the drum and the fife, and now had he rather hear the tabor and the pipe. I have known when he would have walked ten mile afoot to see a good armor, and
15   now will he lie ten nights awake carving the fashion of a new doublet. He was wont to speak plain and to the purpose, like an honest man and a soldier, and now is he turned orthography; his words are a very fantastical banquet, just so many strange dishes. May I be so converted and see with
20   these eyes? I cannot tell; I think not.

ACT 2, SCENE 3

BENEDICK *enters.*

BENEDICK

Boy!

A BOY *enters.*

BOY

Yes Signior?

BENEDICK

In my bedroom window there is a book. Go get it and bring it to me here in the orchard.

BOY

I'm already here, sir.

BENEDICK

The boy means, "It's as good as done," but Benedick plays as if he takes the boy literally.

I see that you are here, but I'd like you to go there and then come back again.

The BOY *exits.*

I'm amazed that a man, after watching romance turn another man into a fool and laughing at that man, can turn right around and become the thing he's scorned. That's the kind of man Claudio is. I knew him when he listened to nothing but the military drum and fife; now he would rather hear the sweet and refined music of the tabor and pipe. I knew him when he would've walked ten miles to see a well-crafted suit of armor; now he spends ten nights awake in his room designing himself a fancy new jacket. He used to speak plainly and to the point, like an honorable man and soldier; now his speech is elaborate and flowery. His words are like a miraculous banquet, full of strange new dishes. Will I be changed like that, and see the world through a lover's eyes? I'm not sure, but I don't think so.

I will not be sworn but love may transform me to an oyster,
but I'll take my oath on it, till he have made an oyster of me,
he shall never make me such a fool. One woman is fair, yet
I am well; another is wise, yet I am well; another virtuous,
yet I am well; but till all graces be in one woman, one
woman shall not come in my grace. Rich she shall be, that's
certain; wise, or I'll none; virtuous, or I'll never cheapen
her; fair, or I'll never look on her; mild, or come not near
me; noble, or not I for an angel; of good discourse, an
excellent musician, and her hair shall be of what color it
please God. Ha! The Prince and Monsieur Love! I will hide
me in the arbor.

He hides

Enter DON PEDRO, CLAUDIO, *and* LEONATO, *and* BALTHASAR
with music

DON PEDRO
Come, shall we hear this music?

CLAUDIO
Yea, my good lord. How still the evening is,
As hushed on purpose to grace harmony!

DON PEDRO
(aside to CLAUDIO*)*
See you where Benedick hath hid himself?

CLAUDIO
(aside to DON PEDRO*)*
O, very well, my lord. The music ended,
We'll fit the kid-fox with a pennyworth.

DON PEDRO
Come, Balthasar, we'll hear that song again.

I can't promise that love won't transform me, but I can promise you this: until I truly fall in love, a woman will never make me act like such a fool. A beautiful woman comes along, but I'm unmoved. A wise woman turns up, but I'm unmoved. A virtuous woman appears, but I'm unmoved. I refuse to fall in love until all three qualities unite in a single woman. She must be rich, certainly, and smart, or I'll have nothing to do with her. She has to be virtuous, or I'll never bid on her; beautiful, or I won't bother to look at her. Mild-mannered, or else she should stay away from me. Noble, or I won't have her even if she's an angel. She must be well spoken, an excellent musician, and her hair should be—well, I suppose the color doesn't matter. Ha! Look, it's the Prince and Mr. Love. I'll hide in the arbor.

He hides.

DON PEDRO, CLAUDIO, *and* LEONATO *enter.* BALTHASAR *enters with music.*

DON PEDRO

Well, should we hear some music?

CLAUDIO

Yes, my lord. Listen to how quiet the evening is, as if it's purposefully setting the stage for a song.

DON PEDRO

(speaking so that only CLAUDIO *can hear)* Do you see where Benedick is hiding?

CLAUDIO

(speaking so that only DON PEDRO *can hear)* Yes, very well, my lord. Once the music has ended, we'll give him more than he bargained for.

DON PEDRO

Come on, Balthasar, let's hear that song again.

BALTHASAR

40   O, good my lord, tax not so bad a voice
        To slander music anymore than once.

DON PEDRO

        It is the witness still of excellency
        To put a strange face on his own perfection.
        I pray thee, sing, and let me woo no more.

BALTHASAR

45   Because you talk of wooing, I will sing,
        Since many a wooer doth commence his suit
        To her he thinks not worthy, yet he woos,
        Yet will he swear he loves.

DON PEDRO

                                    Nay, pray thee, come,
        Or, if thou wilt hold longer argument,
50   Do it in notes.

BALTHASAR

                        Note this before my notes:
        There's not a note of mine that's worth the noting.

DON PEDRO

        Why, these are very crotchets that he speaks!
        Note notes, forsooth, and nothing.

        Music plays

BENEDICK

        (aside) Now, divine air! Now is his soul ravished. Is it not
55   strange that sheeps' guts should hale souls out of men's
        bodies? Well, a horn for my money, when all's done.

BALTHASAR

Oh, my good lord, don't make me insult music again with my awful singing.

DON PEDRO

You can tell an artist is excellent when he denies his own perfection. Please, sing for us; don't make me woo you anymore!

BALTHASAR

Since you put it that way, I'll sing. You're like a suitor who courts a woman insincerely, swearing that he loves her even though he really doesn't find her worthy.

DON PEDRO

Come on, please sing. If you'd like to continue this discussion, at least do so with music.

BALTHASAR

Just know this before I begin: I can't play a single note that's worthy of note.

DON PEDRO

Listen to him speaking in quarter notes! Get on with your note-playing now.

Music plays.

BENEDICK

(to himself) That music must be divine, because their souls have been captivated. Isn't it strange that strings made of sheep's guts are capable of drawing men's souls out of their bodies? Well, *I'd* rather listen to a plain old hunting horn than this music, when all is said and done.

BALTHASAR
> *(singing)*
>> Sigh no more, ladies, sigh no more,
>> Men were deceivers ever,
>> One foot in sea and one on shore,
>> To one thing constant never.
>> Then sigh not so, but let them go,
>> And be you blithe and bonny,
>> Converting all your sounds of woe
>> Into Hey, nonny nonny.
>> Sing no more ditties, sing no mo
>> Of dumps so dull and heavy.
>> The fraud of men was ever so,
>> Since summer first was leavy.
>> Then sigh not so, but let them go
>> And be you blithe and bonny,
>> Converting all your sounds of woe
>> Into Hey, nonny nonny.

DON PEDRO
> By my troth, a good song.

BALTHASAR
> And an ill singer, my lord.

DON PEDRO
> Ha, no, no, faith, thou sing'st well enough for a shift.

BENEDICK
> *(aside)* An he had been a dog that should have howled thus, they would have hanged him. And I pray God his bad voice bode no mischief. I had as lief have heard the night raven, come what plague could have come after it.

DON PEDRO
> Yea, marry, dost thou hear, Balthasar? I pray thee, get us some excellent music, for tomorrow night we would have it at the Lady Hero's chamber window.

BALTHASAR

> *(singing)*
> Don't cry anymore, ladies, don't cry anymore
> Men have always been deceivers,
> One foot on a ship and one on the shore,
> Never devoted to anything.
> So don't cry like that, just let them go,
> And be happy and carefree forever,
> Turning all your sad sounds around
> When you sing "Hey, nonny nonny" instead.
> Don't sing more sad songs
> About being down in the dumps
> For men have been committing this kind of fraud
> Ever since the first summer trees had leaves.
> So don't cry like that, just let them go
> And be happy and carefree forever,
> Turning all your sad sounds around
> When you sing "Hey, nonny nonny" instead.

DON PEDRO

That's a good song.

BALTHASAR

And a bad singer, my lord.

DON PEDRO

Ha! No, no, really, your voice is good enough in a pinch.

BENEDICK

(to himself) If a dog had howled like that, I would have hung it. I hope his horrible singing doesn't have any ill effects. I would've rather listened to the night raven screech, even if the bird's noise does give me the plague, as they say it will.

DON PEDRO

Yes, do you hear me, Balthasar? Please, get some excellent music, because tomorrow we want to serenade Lady Hero at her bedroom window.

BALTHASAR
> The best I can, my lord.

DON PEDRO
> Do so. Farewell.

> *Exit* BALTHASAR

85   Come hither, Leonato. What was it you told me of today,
> that your niece Beatrice was in love with Signor Benedick?

CLAUDIO
> Oh, ay. *(aside to* DON PEDRO*)* Stalk on, stalk on; the fowl
> sits.—I did never think that lady would have loved any
> man.

LEONATO
90   No, nor I neither, but most wonderful that she should so
> dote on Signor Benedick, whom she hath in all outward
> behaviors seemed ever to abhor.

BENEDICK
> *(aside)* Is 't possible? Sits the wind in that corner?

LEONATO
> By my troth, my lord, I cannot tell what to think of it, but
95   that she loves him with an enraged affection, it is past the
> infinite of thought.

DON PEDRO
> May be she doth but counterfeit.

CLAUDIO
> Faith, like enough.

LEONATO
> O God! Counterfeit? There was never counterfeit of
100   passion came so near the life of passion as she discovers it.

DON PEDRO
> Why, what effects of passion shows she?

CLAUDIO
> *(aside to* LEONATO*)* Bait the hook well; this fish will bite.

NO FEAR SHAKESPEARE

BALTHASAR

I'll do the best I can, my lord.

DON PEDRO

Please do. Goodbye.

BALTHASAR exits.

Come here, Leonato. What was it that you told me today—that your niece Beatrice was in love with Signior Benedick?

CLAUDIO

Oh yes. *(speaking so that only* DON PEDRO *can hear)* Go on, keep walking: our prey is in sight.—I never thought that woman would love any man.

LEONATO

I didn't, either. But how wonderful that she should be so fond of Signior Benedick, whom she has always appeared to hate.

BENEDICK

(to himself) Is it possible? Is that the way the wind is blowing?

LEONATO

Really, my lord, I don't know what to make of it, but she loves him with such a passion that it's past all understanding.

DON PEDRO

Maybe she's just pretending.

CLAUDIO

Yes, that's quite likely.

LEONATO

Oh God! Pretending? No one has ever faked passion as skillfully as this, then.

DON PEDRO

Why, what symptoms of love does she exhibit?

CLAUDIO

(speaking so that only LEONATO *can hear)* Bait the hook well; this fish is going to bite.

LEONATO
What effects, my lord? She will sit you—you heard my daughter tell you how.

CLAUDIO
105   She did indeed.

DON PEDRO
How, how I pray you? You amaze me. I would have thought her spirit had been invincible against all assaults of affection.

LEONATO
I would have sworn it had, my lord, especially against Benedick.

BENEDICK
110   *(aside)* I should think this a gull but that the white-bearded fellow speaks it. Knavery cannot, sure, hide himself in such reverence.

CLAUDIO
(aside to DON PEDRO*)* He hath ta'en th' infection. Hold it up.

DON PEDRO
Hath she made her affection known to Benedick?

LEONATO
115   No, and swears she never will. That's her torment.

CLAUDIO
'Tis true indeed, so your daughter says. "Shall I," says she, "that have so oft encountered him with scorn, write to him that I love him?"

LEONATO
This says she now when she is beginning to write to him, for
120   she'll be up twenty times a night, and there will she sit in her smock till she have writ a sheet of paper. My daughter tells us all.

CLAUDIO
Now you talk of a sheet of paper, I remember a pretty jest your daughter told.

LEONATO

> What symptoms, my lord? She will have a seat—you heard my daughter tell you how.

CLAUDIO

> Yes, she did tell us.

DON PEDRO

> Please, please tell me! This is amazing. I would have thought she was invincible against any assault of love.

LEONATO

> I would have sworn that, too, my lord, especially against Benedick.

BENEDICK

> *(to himself)* I would take this as a joke if the old man weren't saying it. Mischief surely can't be hiding in such a respectable man.

CLAUDIO

> *(speaking so that only* DON PEDRO *can hear)* We've infected him! Keep it up.

DON PEDRO

> Has she told Benedick how she feels?

LEONATO

> No, and she swears she never will. That's what's driving her crazy.

CLAUDIO

> It's true, Hero says so. Beatrice asks, "Does it make any sense to write and tell him I love him when I have always treated him with scorn?"

LEONATO

> She says this as she begins to write the letter. She'll be getting up twenty times in a night, sitting there in her slip until she's written a page. My daughter told me everything.

CLAUDIO

> Now that you speak of paper, I remember a funny story of Hero's.

LEONATO

125   Oh, when she had writ it and was reading it over, she found
        "Benedick" and "Beatrice" between the sheet?

CLAUDIO

        That.

LEONATO

        O, she tore the letter into a thousand halfpence, railed at
        herself that she should be so immodest to write to one that
130   she knew would flout her. "I measure him," says she, "by
        my own spirit, for I should flout him if he writ to me, yea,
        though I love him, I should."

CLAUDIO

        Then down upon her knees she falls, weeps, sobs, beats her
        heart, tears her hair, prays, curses: "O sweet Benedick! God
135   give me patience!"

LEONATO

        She doth indeed, my daughter says so, and the ecstasy hath
        so much overborne her that my daughter is sometime
        afeared
        she will do a desperate outrage to herself. It is very true.

DON PEDRO

        It were good that Benedick knew of it by some other, if she
140   will not discover it.

CLAUDIO

        To what end? He would make but a sport of it and torment
        the poor lady worse.

DON PEDRO

        An he should, it were an alms to hang him. She's an
        excellent sweet lady, and, out of all suspicion, she is
145   virtuous.

CLAUDIO

        And she is exceeding wise.

DON PEDRO

        In every thing but in loving Benedick.

LEONATO

Oh, you mean when Beatrice writes a letter and Hero sees that it has "Benedick" and "Beatrice" written all over it?

CLAUDIO

Yes, that's the one.

LEONATO

Oh, she tears that letter into a thousand small pieces and berates herself for being so forward as to write a letter to a man she knows would mock her. "I compare him," she says, "to myself, and I know that I would mock him if he wrote me such a letter. Yes, even though I love him, I would mock him."

CLAUDIO

Then she falls down to her knees, weeps, sobs, beats her breast, tears her hair, prays, and curses: "Oh sweet Benedick! God give me patience!"

LEONATO

She did indeed, my daughter says so. She worries that Beatrice is so overwrought that she might do herself harm someday. It's true.

DON PEDRO

If she won't tell Benedick, someone else should.

CLAUDIO

And what would that accomplish? He'll just turn it into a joke and torment the poor woman even more.

DON PEDRO

If he did that, it would be a charitable deed to hang him. She's an excellent, sweet woman, and there's no doubt that she is virtuous.

CLAUDIO

And she is very smart.

DON PEDRO

Except for the fact that she loves Benedick.

LEONATO
Oh, my lord, wisdom and blood combating in so tender a
body, we have ten proofs to one that blood hath the victory.
150   I am sorry for her, as I have just cause, being her uncle and
her guardian.

DON PEDRO
I would she had bestowed this dotage on me. I would have
daffed all other respects and made her half myself. I pray
you tell Benedick of it and hear what he will say.

LEONATO
155   Were it good, think you?

CLAUDIO
Hero thinks surely she will die, for she says she will die if he
love her not, and she will die ere she make her love known,
and she will die if he woo her rather than she will bate one
breath of her accustomed crossness.

DON PEDRO
160   She doth well. If she should make tender of her love, 'tis
very possible he'll scorn it, for the man, as you know all,
hath a contemptible spirit.

CLAUDIO
He is a very proper man.

DON PEDRO
He hath indeed a good outward happiness.

CLAUDIO
165   Before God, and in my mind, very wise.

DON PEDRO
He doth indeed show some sparks that are like wit.

CLAUDIO
And I take him to be valiant.

DON PEDRO
As Hector, I assure you, and in the managing of quarrels
you may say he is wise, for either he avoids them with great
170   discretion or undertakes them with a most Christian-like
fear.

LEONATO

Oh, my lord, when wisdom and passion are in one body, it's ten to one that the passion will win. I am sorry for her, as I should be, since I am both her uncle and her guardian.

DON PEDRO

I wish she were in love with me instead. I would have thrown away all other considerations and made her my wife. Please, tell Benedick about her feelings and see what he has to say.

LEONATO

Is that a good idea, do you think?

CLAUDIO

Hero thinks Beatrice will surely die, for she says she'll die if he doesn't love her, and that she'll die before she tells him, and she'll die if he woos her and she's made to hold back even one of her usual insults.

DON PEDRO

She's probably right. If she offers him her love, it's very possible that he'll scorn it, since, as we all know, he tends to be contemptuous.

CLAUDIO

He's a very proper man.

DON PEDRO

Indeed, he is good-looking and carries himself well.

CLAUDIO

And I swear to God he's very smart.

DON PEDRO

He does indeed show sparks of something like wit.

CLAUDIO

And I believe him to be brave.

DON PEDRO

Hector was a Trojan warrior, legendary for his bravery.

As brave as Hector, surely. And you could say that he is wise in managing fights, for he either avoids them discreetly or enters into them timidly.

LEONATO

If he do fear God, he must necessarily keep peace. If he break the peace, he ought to enter into a quarrel with fear and trembling.

DON PEDRO

175 And so will he do, for the man doth fear God, howsoever it seems not in him by some large jests he will make. Well, I am sorry for your niece. Shall we go seek Benedick and tell him of her love?

CLAUDIO

Never tell him, my lord, let her wear it out with good
180 counsel.

LEONATO

Nay, that's impossible. She may wear her heart out first.

DON PEDRO

Well, we will hear further of it by your daughter. Let it cool the while. I love Benedick well, and I could wish he would modestly examine himself to see how much he is unworthy
185 so good a lady.

LEONATO

My lord, will you walk? Dinner is ready.

CLAUDIO

(aside to DON PEDRO *and* LEONATO*)* If he do not dote on her upon this, I will never trust my expectation.

DON PEDRO

(aside to LEONATO*)* Let there be the same net spread for her,
190 and that must your daughter and her gentlewomen carry. The sport will be when they hold one an opinion of another's dotage, and no such matter. That's the scene that I would see, which will be merely a dumb show. Let us send her to call him in to dinner.

Exeunt DON PEDRO, CLAUDIO, *and* LEONATO

LEONATO

If he fears God, he must necessarily keep the peace. If he breaks the peace, he ought to enter into a quarrel with fear and trembling.

DON PEDRO

And he'll do that, because he's a God-fearing man, even though his joking makes it seem otherwise. Well, I'm sorry for your niece. Should we go find Benedick and tell him about Beatrice's love?

CLAUDIO

No, don't ever tell him, my lord. Let her get over it, with the help of good advice.

LEONATO

No, that's impossible. Her heart will break first.

DON PEDRO

Well, we'll hear more about it from your daughter. Let it sit for a while. I am very fond of Benedick, and I just wish he would take a look at himself and realize how unfairly he's treating this good woman.

LEONATO

My lord, will you come with me? Dinner is ready.

CLAUDIO

(speaking so that only DON PEDRO *and* LEONATO *can hear)* If he doesn't fall in love with her now, I'll never trust my intuition again.

DON PEDRO

(speaking so that only LEONATO *can hear)* The same trap must be set for her; that's your daughter's and servants' job. The real fun will be when they both believe the other to be in love, without any of it being true. I can't wait to watch that drama—it'll be a pantomime, since both of them will be totally speechless! Let's send Beatrice to call Benedick in to dinner.

Everyone except BENEDICK *exits.*

BENEDICK

195   *(coming forward)* This can be no trick. The conference was
        sadly borne; they have the truth of this from Hero; they
        seem to pity the lady. It seems her affections have their full
        bent. Love me? Why, it must be requited! I hear how I am
        censured. They say I will bear myself proudly if I perceive
200   the love come from her. They say, too, that she will rather
        die than give any sign of affection. I did never think to
        marry. I must not seem proud. Happy are they that hear
        their detractions and can put them to mending. They say
        the lady is fair; 'tis a truth, I can bear them witness. And
205   virtuous; 'tis so, I cannot reprove it. And wise, but for
        loving me; by my troth, it is no addition to her wit, nor no
        great argument of her folly, for I will be horribly in love
        with her! I may chance have some odd quirks and remnants
        of wit broken on me because I have railed so long against
210   marriage, but doth not the appetite alter? A man loves the
        meat in his youth that he cannot endure in his age. Shall
        quips and sentences and these paper bullets of the brain
        awe a man from the career of his humor?
        No! The world must be peopled. When I said I would die a
215   bachelor, I did not think I should live till I were married.
        Here comes Beatrice. By this day, she's a fair lady. I do spy
        some marks of love in her.

        Enter **BEATRICE**

BEATRICE

Against my will, I am sent to bid you come in to dinner.

BENEDICK

Fair Beatrice, I thank you for your pains.

BENEDICK

(coming forward) This can't be a trick. They spoke with great seriousness, and they have Hero's testimony. They seem to pity the lady. It seems her love is stretched to the limit. She loves me? Well, that love must be returned! I hear how I'm criticized. They say I'll be smug if I find out she loves me. They also say she'd rather die than give any sign of her feelings. I never thought I'd marry. I can't appear to be proud. People who discover their faults and can then change them are lucky indeed. They say the lady is beautiful; it's true, I've seen it myself. And virtuous; that's true, I can't disprove that. And smart, except that she loves me. That may not be any proof of her intelligence, but I swear it won't be evidence of her stupidity—for I'm going to be horribly in love with her! People might tease me here and there, since I attacked marriage for so long. But don't tastes change? A man can love a dish when he is young that he hates when he turns old. Will quips and clever remarks and scathing written words keep a man from getting what his heart desires? No! The world needs to be populated. When I said that I'd die as a bachelor, I just meant that I didn't think I'd live until I got married. Here comes Beatrice. By God! She's a beautiful lady. I think I sense some signs of love in her.

BEATRICE *enters.*

BEATRICE

Against my will, I've been told to bring you in to dinner.

BENEDICK

Lovely Beatrice, I thank you for taking the pains to tell me that.

BEATRICE

220   I took no more pains for those thanks than you take pains to
thank me. If it had been painful, I would not have come.

BENEDICK

You take pleasure then in the message?

BEATRICE

Yea, just so much as you may take upon a knife's point and
choke a daw withal. You have no stomach, Signior. Fare you
225   well.

Exit

BENEDICK

Ha! "Against my will I am sent to bid you come in to
dinner." There's a double meaning in that. "I took no more
pains for those thanks than you took pains to thank me."
That's as much as to say, "Any pains that I take for you is as
230   easy as thanks." If I do not take pity of her, I am a villain.
If I do not love her, I am a Jew. I will go get her picture.

Exit

BEATRICE

I didn't take any more pains bringing this message than you took pains in thanking me. If the job had been painful, I would not have come.

BENEDICK

So you took pleasure in bringing me this message?

BEATRICE

Yes, as much pleasure as one might take in choking a bird at knifepoint. You don't want to eat, sir? Goodbye, then.

She exits.

BENEDICK

Ha! "Against my will, I've been told to bring you in to dinner." There's a double meaning in that. "I didn't take any more pains bringing this message than you took pains in thanking me." That's like saying, "Anything I do for you is as easy as saying 'thank you.'" If this doesn't move me to take pity on her, I'm a horrible person. If I don't love her, I'm completely hardhearted. I will go get her picture.

According to anti-Semitic stereotypes, Jews were supposed to be hard-hearted and lacking a sense of charity.

He exits.

ACT THREE

SCENE 1

Enter HERO, MARGARET, *and* URSULA

HERO
Good Margaret, run thee to the parlor.
There shalt thou find my cousin Beatrice
Proposing with the Prince and Claudio.
Whisper her ear and tell her I and Ursula
5   Walk in the orchard, and our whole discourse
Is all of her. Say that thou overheardst us,
And bid her steal into the pleachèd bower
Where honeysuckles ripened by the sun
Forbid the sun to enter, like favorites
10   Made proud by princes, that advance their pride
Against that power that bred it. There will she hide her
To listen our propose. This is thy office.
Bear thee well in it and leave us alone.

MARGARET
I'll make her come, I warrant you, presently.

Exit

HERO
15   Now, Ursula, when Beatrice doth come,
As we do trace this alley up and down,
Our talk must only be of Benedick.
When I do name him, let it be thy part
To praise him more than ever man did merit.
20   My talk to thee must be how Benedick
Is sick in love with Beatrice. Of this matter
Is little Cupid's crafty arrow made,
That only wounds by hearsay.

Enter BEATRICE, *behind*

ACT THREE

SCENE 1

HERO, MARGARET, *and* URSULA *enter.*

HERO

Margaret, run into the sitting room. You'll find Beatrice there, talking to Claudio and the Prince. Whisper to her that Ursula and I are walking in the orchard and that we're talking all about her. Tell her you heard us, and that she should sneak into the arbor where the crisscrossing branches overhead keep the honeysuckles out of the sun. (The same honeysuckles that were once ripened in the sun; they're like courtiers who rise because the king favors them, then plot to overthrow his Majesty.) She can hide there and eavesdrop on our conversation. This is your job. Do it well, and then leave us.

MARGARET

I'll make her come right away, I promise you.

She exits.

HERO

All right Ursula, as Beatrice arrives, we'll be walking up and down this alley and speaking about nothing but Benedick. Whenever I mention him, praise him more than any man deserves. It'll be my job to talk about how Benedick is sick with love for Beatrice. We'll make our arrows the same way Cupid does: with gossip and rumor.

BEATRICE *enters, behind.*

                                    Now begin,
    For look where Beatrice like a lapwing runs
25   Close by the ground, to hear our conference.

URSULA
    (aside to HERO*)*
    The pleasant'st angling is to see the fish
    Cut with her golden oars the silver stream
    And greedily devour the treacherous bait.
    So angle we for Beatrice, who even now
30   Is couchèd in the woodbine coverture.
    Fear you not my part of the dialogue.

HERO
    (aside to URSULA*)*
    Then go we near her, that her ear lose nothing
    Of the false sweet bait that we lay for it.—
    (approaching the bower)
    No, truly, Ursula, she is too disdainful.
35   I know her spirits are as coy and wild
    As haggards of the rock.

URSULA
                    But are you sure
    That Benedick loves Beatrice so entirely?

HERO
    So says the Prince and my new-trothèd lord.

URSULA
    And did they bid you tell her of it, madam?

HERO
40   They did entreat me to acquaint her of it,
    But I persuaded them, if they loved Benedick,
    To wish him wrestle with affection
    And never to let Beatrice know of it.

URSULA
    Why did you so? Doth not the gentleman
45   Deserve as full as fortunate a bed
    As ever Beatrice shall couch upon?

Let's start. See, Beatrice has run over like a little bird,
keeping close to the ground and trying to overhear us.

URSULA

(speaking so that only HERO *can hear)* The best part of
fishing is watching the fish cut through the water and
greedily take the bait. Now we're fishing for Beatrice,
who's hiding right now in the honeysuckle arbor.
Don't worry, I'll do my part.

HERO

(speaking so that only URSULA *can hear)* Then let's get
closer, so she can hear all the false, sweet bait we're
setting for her.— *(approaching the bower)* No, truly,
Ursula, she's too scornful. She's as devious and fierce
as the wild hawks on the rocks.

URSULA

But are you sure that Benedick loves Beatrice that
much?

HERO

That's what the Prince and my fiancé say.

URSULA

And did they ask you to tell Beatrice about this, madam?

HERO

They did want me to tell her, but I persuaded them
that, if they truly loved Benedick, they would try to
get him to battle his emotions and keep Beatrice in the
dark.

URSULA

Why did you do that? Doesn't Benedick deserve as
much luck with a mate as he would have with Beatrice?

HERO

O god of love! I know he doth deserve
As much as may be yielded to a man,
But Nature never framed a woman's heart
50   Of prouder stuff than that of Beatrice.
Disdain and scorn ride sparkling in her eyes,
Misprizing what they look on, and her wit
Values itself so highly that to her
All matter else seems weak. She cannot love
55   Nor take no shape nor project of affection
She is so self-endeared.

URSULA

                              Sure, I think so,
And therefore certainly it were not good
She knew his love, lest she make sport at it.

HERO

Why, you speak truth. I never yet saw man,
60   How wise, how noble, young, how rarely featured
But she would spell him backward. If fair-faced,
She would swear the gentleman should be her sister;
If black, why, Nature, drawing of an antic,
Made a foul blot; if tall, a lance ill-headed;
65   If low, an agate very vilely cut;
If speaking, why, a vane blown with all winds;
If silent, why, a block moved with none.
So turns she every man the wrong side out
And never gives to truth and virtue that
70   Which simpleness and merit purchaseth.

URSULA

Sure, sure, such carping is not commendable.

HERO

No, not to be so odd and from all fashions
As Beatrice is, cannot be commendable.
But who dare tell her so? If I should speak,
75   She would mock me into air. O, she would laugh me
Out of myself, press me to death with wit.

HERO

By the god of love, I know that he deserves all that a man might possess. But Nature never made a woman's heart as proud and tough as Beatrice's. There is scorn and disdain in her eyes, and those sparkling eyes despise everything they look upon. She values her wit more highly than anything else, which looks weak by comparison. She's so in love with herself, she's incapable of loving anyone else. She can't even imagine what "love" is.

URSULA

Yes, you're right. It would be bad if she knew about Benedick's love and teased him about it.

HERO

It's true. Whenever she meets a man—no matter how wise, noble, young, handsome—she rearranges all his good qualities so they end up looking bad. If he has a fair complexion, she'll say the pretty man should be her sister, not her husband. If he's dark-skinned, Nature must have spilled some ink while drawing his foolish face. If he's tall, she'll say he's a spear topped by an odd head; if he's short, she says he looks like a badly carved miniature. If he's talkative, he's a weathervane, moving in all directions at once; if he's silent, he's a block that can't be moved at all. And so she turns men inside out and never acknowledges the integrity and merit that a man has.

URSULA

It's true, her nitpicking is hardly admirable.

HERO

No, it certainly is not admirable to be so perverse and eccentric. But who would dare tell her? If I said something, she'd mock me so mercilessly that I'd probably disintegrate into air. She'd laugh me right out of my body and kill me with her wit.

Therefore let Benedick, like covered fire,
Consume away in sighs, waste inwardly.
It were a better death than die with mocks,
80   Which is as bad as die with tickling.

URSULA
Yet tell her of it. Hear what she will say.

HERO
No, rather I will go to Benedick
And counsel him to fight against his passion;
And truly I'll devise some honest slanders
85   To stain my cousin with. One doth not know
How much an ill word may empoison liking.

URSULA
O, do not do your cousin such a wrong!
She cannot be so much without true judgment,
Having so swift and excellent a wit
90   As she is prized to have, as to refuse
So rare a gentleman as Signior Benedick.

HERO
He is the only man of Italy,
Always excepted my dear Claudio.

URSULA
I pray you, be not angry with me, madam,
95   Speaking my fancy. Signor Benedick,
For shape, for bearing, argument and valor,
Goes foremost in report through Italy.

HERO
Indeed, he hath an excellent good name.

URSULA
His excellence did earn it, ere he had it.
100   When are you married, madam?

So Benedick should conceal his emotions. Like a fire that gets covered up, Benedick should smother his love and waste away. It would be better to die that way than to die from being mocked, which is as bad as being killed by tickling.

URSULA

But you should tell her about this, and hear what she has to say.

HERO

No, instead I'll go to Benedick and advise him to fight his emotions. I'll make up some awful things about my cousin and ruin her reputation. You don't know how quickly affection can be killed with a single nasty word.

URSULA

Oh, don't injure your cousin like that! With the quick, intelligent wit she's rumored to have, she can't really be such a bad judge of character that she'd refuse a man as exceptional as Signior Benedick.

HERO

He's the only worthy man in Italy, aside from my dear Claudio.

URSULA

Don't be angry with me for speaking my mind, but throughout Italy, Benedick is considered the best man in looks, bearing, intelligence, and bravery.

HERO

True, he has an excellent reputation.

URSULA

And he deserves it, having been excellent before he had a reputation for it. When are you getting married, madam?

HERO
> Why, every day, tomorrow. Come, go in.
> I'll show thee some attires, and have thy counsel
> Which is the best to furnish me tomorrow.

They move aside from the bower

URSULA
> *(aside to HERO)*
105   She's limed, I warrant you. We have caught her, madam.

HERO
> *(aside to URSULA)*
> If it proves so, then loving goes by haps;
> Some Cupid kills with arrows, some with traps.

Exeunt HERO and URSULA

BEATRICE
> *(coming forward)*
> What fire is in mine ears? Can this be true?
> Stand I condemned for pride and scorn so much?
110   Contempt, farewell, and maiden pride, adieu!
> No glory lives behind the back of such.
> And Benedick, love on; I will requite thee,
> Taming my wild heart to thy loving hand.
> If thou dost love, my kindness shall incite thee
115   To bind our loves up in a holy band.
> For others say thou dost deserve, and I
> Believe it better than reportingly.

Exit

HERO

Tomorrow, and then every day after that. Come on, let's go inside. I want to show you some clothing, so you can tell me what I should wear tomorrow.

They move away from the bower.

URSULA

(speaking so that only HERO *can hear)* We caught her in our trap, madam, I'm sure of it.

HERO

(speaking so that only URSULA *can hear)* If so, then you never know where love will come from. Cupid gets some lovers with arrows, but some he lays traps for!

Everyone but BEATRICE *exits.*

BEATRICE

(coming forward) I'm burning up with shame! Can this be true? Do people criticize me this much for being proud and scornful? Then I'll say goodbye to my contempt and my pride in being unmarried! No good is spoken of such a person as me behind her back. Benedick, keep on loving me and I will return your love, like a wild hawk being tamed by her handler. I'll be kind to you from now on, and if you really do love me, that kindness will encourage you to seal our love with a wedding band. People say that you deserve my love, and I believe it—not just because they've said so.

She exits.

ACT 3, SCENE 2

Enter DON PEDRO, CLAUDIO, BENEDICK, *and* LEONATO

DON PEDRO
I do but stay till your marriage be consummate, and then go
I toward Aragon.

CLAUDIO
I'll bring you thither, my lord, if you'll vouchsafe me.

DON PEDRO
Nay, that would be as great a soil in the new gloss of your
5   marriage as to show a child his new coat and forbid him to
wear it. I will only be bold with Benedick for his company,
for from the crown of his head to the sole of his foot he is all
mirth. He hath twice or thrice cut Cupid's bow-string, and
the little hangman dare not shoot at him. He hath a heart as
10   sound as a bell, and his tongue is the clapper, for what his
heart thinks, his tongue speaks.

BENEDICK
Gallants, I am not as I have been.

LEONATO
So say I. Methinks you are sadder.

CLAUDIO
I hope he be in love.

DON PEDRO
15   Hang him, truant! There's no true drop of blood in him to
be truly touched with love. If he be sad, he wants money.

BENEDICK
I have the toothache.

DON PEDRO
Draw it.

BENEDICK
Hang it!

CLAUDIO
20   You must hang it first, and draw it afterwards.

ACT 3, SCENE 2

DON PEDRO, CLAUDIO, BENEDICK, *and* LEONATO *enter.*

DON PEDRO

I'll stay in Messina until you're married, and then I'll go to Aragon.

CLAUDIO

I'll go with you, my lord, if you'll allow me.

DON PEDRO

No, taking you away from your new marriage would be like showing a child a new coat and then not letting him wear it. I'll ask only Benedick to come with me, for from the top of his head to the soles of his feet he's a joker. He's evaded love once or twice, and since then Cupid doesn't dare to shoot at him. Benedick's heart is like a bell, with his tongue as the clapper: everything his heart thinks, his tongue speaks.

BENEDICK

Gentleman, I am not the same man I was before.

LEONATO

I agree. I think you seem more serious.

CLAUDIO

I hope he's in love.

DON PEDRO

Come off it, man! There isn't a single drop of sincerity in him that could be touched with love. If he looks serious, he must need money.

BENEDICK

I have a toothache.

> Toothache was an ailment associated with lovers.

DON PEDRO

> "Pull it out."

Draw it.

BENEDICK

Hang it!

> An expression of impatience.

CLAUDIO

> Claudio plays on the fact that criminals were hanged and then "drawn," or disemboweled.

You have to hang it first. Then you can draw it.

DON PEDRO
What, sigh for the toothache?

LEONATO
Where is but a humor or a worm.

BENEDICK
Well, everyone can master a grief but he that has it.

CLAUDIO
Yet say I, he is in love.

DON PEDRO
25   There is no appearance of fancy in him, unless it be a fancy
that he hath to strange disguises, as to be a Dutchman
today, a Frenchman tomorrow, or in the shape of two
countries at once, as a German from the waist downward,
all slops, and a Spaniard from the hip upward, no doublet.
30   Unless he have a fancy to this foolery, as it appears he hath,
he is no fool for fancy, as you would have it appear he is.

CLAUDIO
If he be not in love with some woman, there is no believing
old signs. He brushes his hat o' mornings. What should
that bode?

DON PEDRO
35   Hath any man seen him at the barber's?

CLAUDIO
No, but the barber's man hath been seen with him, and the
old ornament of his cheek hath already stuffed tennis balls.

LEONATO
Indeed, he looks younger than he did, by the loss of a beard.

DON PEDRO
Nay, he rubs himself with civet. Can you smell him out by
40   that?

DON PEDRO

What, are you moaning on about your toothache?

LEONATO

Most illnesses were attributed to bodily fluids or parasites.

It could only have been caused by some humor or worm.

BENEDICK

Well, everyone knows how to overcome an injury except the one who actually has one.

CLAUDIO

I repeat, he's in love.

DON PEDRO

No, there's no love in him, unless you mean his love for strange costumes. He's a Dutchman today, a Frenchman tomorrow, and sometimes wears the clothing of two countries at once: a German from the waist down, with his baggy pants, and a Spaniard from the hips up, with a cloak and no jacket. Unless you're talking about his love for this kind of foolishness—which, judging from his appearance, he has— he is no fool for love, as you pretend.

CLAUDIO

If he's not in love with a woman, then you can't trust the usual symptoms. He brushes his hat in the mornings. What do you think that means?

DON PEDRO

Has any man seen him at the barber's?

CLAUDIO

Tennis balls used to be stuffed with hair.

No, but the barber's assistant has been seen with him. The beard that used to decorate Benedick's cheeks has been shaved off and is now stuffing tennis balls.

LEONATO

Getting rid of the beard definitely makes him look younger.

DON PEDRO

And he's rubbed himself with perfume. Can you smell out his secret now?

CLAUDIO
> That's as much as to say, the sweet youth's in love.

DON PEDRO
> The greatest note of it is his melancholy.

CLAUDIO
> And when was he wont to wash his face?

DON PEDRO
> Yea, or to paint himself? For the which I hear what they say
45   of him.

CLAUDIO
> Nay, but his jesting spirit, which is now crept into a lute
> string and now governed by stops—

DON PEDRO
> Indeed, that tells a heavy tale for him. Conclude, conclude,
> he is in love.

CLAUDIO
50   Nay, but I know who loves him.

DON PEDRO
> That would I know too. I warrant, one that knows him not.

CLAUDIO
> Yes, and his ill conditions, and, in despite of all, dies for
> him.

DON PEDRO
> She shall be buried with her face upwards.

CLAUDIO

That's as good as proof that the sweet young man's in love.

DON PEDRO

The biggest clue is his seriousness.

CLAUDIO

And when has he ever been known to wash his face?

DON PEDRO

Yes, or to wear cosmetics? I hear what they say about him for doing that.

CLAUDIO

A lute is an instrument used in lovers' serenades.

Indeed, his mocking spirit has now crawled into a lute, and he can be played like an instrument—

DON PEDRO

Truly, it all adds up to a serious story for Benedick. A conclusion, a conclusion: he is in love.

CLAUDIO

Oh, and I know who loves him.

DON PEDRO

I bet I know, too: someone who clearly doesn't know him at all.

CLAUDIO

No, she does know him, and she also knows all his bad qualities—and in spite of all this, she still dies for him.

DON PEDRO

In Shakespeare's time, "to die" was slang for having an orgasm; Don Pedro jokes that the woman will actually die when she "dies"— during sexual intercourse.

She'll be buried with her face upwards, then.

BENEDICK

55   Yet is this no charm for the toothache.—Old Signior, walk aside with me. I have studied eight or nine wise words to speak to you, which these hobbyhorses must not hear.

Exeunt BENEDICK *and* LEONATO

DON PEDRO

     For my life, to break with him about Beatrice!

CLAUDIO

     'Tis even so. Hero and Margaret have by this played their
60   parts with Beatrice, and then the two bears will not bite one another when they meet.

Enter DON JOHN

DON JOHN

     My lord and brother, God save you.

DON PEDRO

     Good e'en, brother.

DON JOHN

     If your leisure served, I would speak with you.

DON PEDRO

65   In private?

DON JOHN

     If it please you. Yet Count Claudio may hear, for what I would speak of concerns him.

DON PEDRO

     What's the matter?

DON JOHN

     (to CLAUDIO*)* Means your lordship to be married tomorrow?

DON PEDRO

70   You know he does.

DON JOHN

     I know not that, when he knows what I know.

NO FEAR SHAKESPEARE

BENEDICK

This chatter is no cure for my toothache. *(to* LEONATO*)* Old sir, please walk with me a bit. I have eight or nine well-considered words to say to you, and I don't want these fools to hear.

BENEDICK and LEONATO exit.

DON PEDRO

I bet my life he's gone to speak with Leonato about Beatrice!

CLAUDIO

It must be. By now, Hero and Margaret have done their part with Beatrice. The two bears won't bite each other the next time they meet.

DON JOHN enters.

DON JOHN

My lord and brother, God save you.

DON PEDRO

Good evening, brother.

DON JOHN

If you don't mind, I'd like to speak with you.

DON PEDRO

In private?

DON JOHN

If you wish. But Count Claudio can stay, for what I'm about to say concerns him.

DON PEDRO

What's the matter?

DON JOHN

(to CLAUDIO*)* Do you plan on getting married tomorrow?

DON PEDRO

You know that he does.

DON JOHN

I don't know that, once he knows what I know.

CLAUDIO
      If there be any impediment, I pray you discover it.

DON JOHN
      You may think I love you not. Let that appear hereafter, and
      aim better at me by that I now will manifest. For my
75   brother, I think he holds you well, and in dearness of heart
      hath holp to effect your ensuing marriage—surely suit ill
      spent and labor ill bestowed.

DON PEDRO
      Why, what's the matter?

DON JOHN
      I came hither to tell you; and, circumstances shortened, for
80   she has been too long a-talking of, the lady is disloyal.

CLAUDIO
      Who, Hero?

DON JOHN
      Even she: Leonato's Hero, your Hero, every man's Hero.

CLAUDIO
      Disloyal?

DON JOHN
      The word is too good to paint out her wickedness. I could
85   say she were worse. Think you of a worse title, and I will fit
      her to it. Wonder not till further warrant. Go but with me
      tonight, you shall see her chamber window entered, even
      the night before her wedding day. If you love her then,
      tomorrow wed her. But it would better fit your honor to
90   change your mind.

CLAUDIO
      (to DON PEDRO*)* May this be so?

DON PEDRO
      I will not think it.

CLAUDIO

If there's any reason we shouldn't get married, I urge you to tell me.

DON JOHN

You may think that I don't love you. I hope that, after I tell you my news, you will think better of me. My brother thinks highly of you, and because of his affection, has helped arrange your marriage—but that was definitely a waste of his time and energy.

DON PEDRO

Why, what's the matter?

DON JOHN

I came here to tell you—I'll make this short, since she's already been talked about for too long—the lady is unfaithful.

CLAUDIO

Who, Hero?

DON JOHN

That's the one: Leonato's Hero, your Hero, every man's Hero.

CLAUDIO

Unfaithful?

DON JOHN

The word is too good to represent her wickedness. She is worse than wicked. If you can think of a more awful title, I'll call her that. But don't keep wondering without more proof. Come with me tonight, and you'll see a man enter her bedroom chamber—even tonight, the night before her wedding. If you still love her after that, then marry her tomorrow. But you would be more honorable if you changed your mind.

CLAUDIO

(to DON PEDRO*)* Is this possible?

DON PEDRO

I won't consider it.

DON JOHN

If you dare not trust that you see, confess not that you know.
If you will follow me, I will show you enough, and when

95   you have seen more and heard more, proceed accordingly.

CLAUDIO

If I see anything tonight why I should not marry her,
tomorrow in the congregation, where I should wed, there
will I shame her.

DON PEDRO

And as I wooed for thee to obtain her, I will join with thee

100   to disgrace her.

DON JOHN

I will disparage her no farther till you are my witnesses.
Bear it coldly but till midnight and let the issue show itself.

DON PEDRO

O day untowardly turned!

CLAUDIO

O mischief strangely thwarting!

DON JOHN

105   O plague right well prevented! So will you say when you
have seen the sequel.

Exeunt

NO FEAR SHAKESPEARE

DON JOHN

If you won't risk coming to see her tonight, then don't claim to know what she's like. If you follow me, I'll give you all the proof you need. Once you have seen more and heard more, then you can decide what to do.

CLAUDIO

If I see anything tonight that convinces me not to marry her, I'll shame her tomorrow in the very congregation where I would have married her.

DON PEDRO

And since I wooed her in your name, I'll join you in disgracing her.

DON JOHN

I won't say anything else about her until you two see things for yourselves. Remain calm until midnight, and then you'll see what the trouble is.

DON PEDRO

Oh, this day has turned into a disaster!

CLAUDIO

Oh, mischief has ruined our plans!

DON JOHN

Oh, a plague has been prevented, thank God! That's what you'll say once you've seen part two.

They all exit.

ACT 3, SCENE 3

Enter DOGBERRY *and* VERGES *with the Watch*

DOGBERRY
Are you good men and true?

VERGES
Yea, or else it were pity but they should suffer salvation,
body and soul.

DOGBERRY
Nay, that were a punishment too good for them, if they
5   should have any allegiance in them, being chosen for the
Prince's watch.

VERGES
Well, give them their charge, neighbor Dogberry.

DOGBERRY
First, who think you the most desartless man to be
constable?

FIRST WATCHMAN
10   Hugh Otecake, sir, or George Seacole, for they can write
and read.

DOGBERRY
Come hither, neighbor Seacole. God hath blessed you with
a good name. To be a well-favored man is the gift of fortune,
but to write and read comes by nature.

SEACOLE
15   Both which, Master Constable—

DOGBERRY
You have. I knew it would be your answer. Well, for your
favor, sir, why, give God thanks, and make no boast of it,
and for your writing and reading, let that appear when there
is no need of such vanity. You are thought here to be the
20   most senseless and fit man for the constable of the watch;
therefore bear you the lantern. This is your charge:

Dogberry and Verges, comically addled characters, continually say the opposite of what they mean.

ACT 3, SCENE 3

DOGBERRY *and* VERGES *with several of the Prince's* WATCHMEN *enter.*

"Watchmen" are officers patrolling the city at night.

DOGBERRY

Are you all good and honest men?

VERGES

By "salvation," he means "damnation."

Yes they are, otherwise it would be proper for them to suffer salvation, body and soul.

DOGBERRY

By "allegiance," he means "disloyalty."

If they had any allegiance when they were chosen for the Prince's watch, a punishment like that would be too good for them.

VERGES

Well, give them their assignment, Sir Dogberry.

DOGBERRY

By "desertless" (a made-up word), he means "deserving."

First, which man do you think is most desertless to be leader of the watch?

FIRST WATCHMAN

Either Hugh Otecake, sir, or else George Seacole, because both of them can read and write.

DOGBERRY

Come here, Sir Seacole. God has blessed you with a good name. To be good-looking is a matter of luck, but to read and write is a natural gift.

SEACOLE

Both of which, master constable—

DOGBERRY

You have. I knew that would be your answer. Well, for your good looks, sir, thank God and don't boast about it. As for your reading and writing, use those skills when you can't use your looks. You're thought to be the most senseless and fit man here, so you will carry the lantern and be constable. This is your assignment:

By "senseless," he means "sensible."

you shall comprehend all vagrom men; you are to bid any
man stand, in the Prince's name.

SEACOLE
How if he will not stand?

DOGBERRY
25   Why, then, take no note of him, but let him go and
presently call the rest of the watch together and thank God
you are rid of a knave.

VERGES
If he will not stand when he is bidden, he is none of the
Prince's subjects.

DOGBERRY
30   True, and they are to meddle with none but the Prince's
subjects.—You shall also make no noise in the streets; for,
for the watch to babble and to talk is most tolerable and not
to be endured.

FIRST WATCHMAN
We will rather sleep than talk. We know what belongs to a
35   watch.

DOGBERRY
Why, you speak like an ancient and most quiet watchman,
for I cannot see how sleeping should offend. Only have a
care that your bills be not stolen. Well, you are to call at all
the alehouses and bid those that are drunk get them to bed.

FIRST WATCHMAN
40   How if they will not?

DOGBERRY
Why, then, let them alone till they are sober. If they make
you not then the better answer, you may say they are not the
men you took them for.

FIRST WATCHMAN
Well, sir.

By "comprehend,"
he means
"apprehend."

you will comprehend any vagrant men you see. You are to order all men to stop, in the Prince's name.

SEACOLE

And what if he won't stop?

DOGBERRY

Well then, don't bother with him and let him go. Then immediately call the rest of the watch together and thank God that you've gotten rid of such a criminal.

VERGES

If he won't stop when he's told to, then he isn't one of the Prince's subjects.

DOGBERRY

True, and you aren't supposed to meddle with anyone but the Prince's subjects. You will also stay quiet in the streets, for a babbling watch is most tolerable and will not be endured.

By "tolerable," he
means "intolerable."

FIRST WATCHMAN

We'll sleep instead of talk. We know what's appropriate for a watch.

DOGBERRY

Why, you speak like an experienced and quiet watchman. Sleeping on the watch shouldn't be a problem; just make sure that your weapons don't get stolen. Also, you're supposed to visit all the bars and tell anyone who's drunk to go home and go to bed.

FIRST WATCHMAN

And what if they won't go?

DOGBERRY

Well then, leave them alone until they're sober. If even then they don't answer to your satisfaction, you can say that they're not the men you thought they were.

FIRST WATCHMAN

Very good, sir.

DOGBERRY

45   If you meet a thief, you may suspect him, by virtue of your
office, to be no true man, and for such kind of men, the less
you meddle or make with them, why the more is for your
honesty.

SEACOLE

If we know him to be a thief, shall we not lay hands on him?

DOGBERRY

50   Truly, by your office you may, but I think they that touch
pitch will be defiled. The most peaceable way for you, if you
do take a thief, is to let him show himself what he is and steal
out of your company.

VERGES

You have been always called a merciful man, partner.

DOGBERRY

55   Truly, I would not hang a dog by my will, much more a man
who hath any honesty in him.

VERGES

(to the Watch) If you hear a child cry in the night, you must
call to the nurse and bid her still it.

SEACOLE

How if the nurse be asleep and will not hear us?

DOGBERRY

60   Why then, depart in peace and let the child wake her with
crying, for the ewe that will not hear her lamb when it baas
will never answer a calf when he bleats.

VERGES

'Tis very true.

DOGBERRY

This is the end of the charge. You, constable, are to present
65   the Prince's own person. If you meet the Prince in the night,
you may stay him.

VERGES

Nay, by 'r Lady, that I think he cannot.

DOGBERRY

If you meet a thief, you can expect him to be dishonest. The less you have to do with that kind of man, the more honest you will be.

SEACOLE

So if we know that a man is a thief, should we try to arrest him?

DOGBERRY

Your position permits you to, but I think that those who stick their hands in pitch get their hands dirty. If you encounter a thief, I think the most peaceable thing to do is to let him be himself—and steal away.

Pitch is a dark, sticky, tar-like substance.

VERGES

You have always been known as a merciful man, partner.

DOGBERRY

Truly, I wouldn't even hang a dog, much more a man who has any honesty in him.

By "more," he means "less."

VERGES

(to the watchmen) If you hear a child crying in the night, you should call the nurse and tell her to quiet the child.

SEACOLE

What if the nurse is asleep and doesn't hear us?

DOGBERRY

Well then, leave quietly, and let the child's crying wake up the nurse. The ewe that doesn't go to her lamb when it *baas* will never tend to another animal's child.

VERGES

That's very true.

DOGBERRY

And that's the end of your assignment. You, constable, are representing the Prince himself. If you meet the Prince in the night, you can order him to stop.

VERGES

No, by our Lady, I don't think he can.

DOGBERRY
Five shillings to one on 't, with any man that knows the
statutes, he may stay him—marry, not without the Prince
70   be willing, for indeed the watch ought to offend no man,
and it is an offense to stay a man against his will.

VERGES
By 'r lady, I think it be so.

DOGBERRY
Ha, ha, ha!—Well, masters, good night. An there be any
matter of weight chances, call up me. Keep your fellows'
75   counsels and your own; and good night.—Come, neighbor.

SEACOLE
Well, masters, we hear our charge. Let us go sit here upon
the church bench till two, and then all to bed.

DOGBERRY
One word more, honest neighbors. I pray you watch about
Signior Leonato's door, for the wedding being there
80   tomorrow, there is a great coil tonight. Adieu, be vigitant,
I beseech you.

Exeunt DOGBERRY *and* VERGES

Enter BORACHIO *and* CONRADE

BORACHIO
What Conrade!

SEACOLE
(aside) Peace! Stir not.

BORACHIO
Conrade, I say!

CONRADE
85   Here, man. I am at thy elbow.

DOGBERRY

I'll bet any man who knows the law five shillings to one on it. Truly though, you can't stop the Prince without the Prince's consent, for the watch shouldn't offend anyone, and it's an offense to keep a man without his consent.

VERGES

By our Lady, I think that's true.

DOGBERRY

Ha, ha, ha! Well, gentlemen, good night. And if anything important happens, find me and let me know. Keep each other's secrets and your own. Good night. Come, friend.

SEACOLE

Well gentlemen, we've heard our assignment. Let's sit here on the church bench until two and then go off to bed.

DOGBERRY

One more thing, good gentlemen. Watch over Signior Leonato's house; with the wedding being held there tomorrow, there's a great to-do there tonight. Adieu. Be vigitant, I beg you.

By "vigitant," he means "vigilant."

> **DOGBERRY** and **VERGES** exit.

> **BORACHIO** and **CONRADE** enter.

BORACHIO

Conrade!

SEACOLE

(whispering) Quiet! Don't move!

BORACHIO

Conrade, I say!

CONRADE

I'm here, man, at your elbow.

BORACHIO
Mass, and my elbow itched, I thought there would a scab follow.

CONRADE
I will owe thee an answer for that. And now forward with thy tale.

BORACHIO
90 Stand thee close, then, under this penthouse, for it drizzles rain, and I will, like a true drunkard, utter all to thee.

SEACOLE
(aside) Some treason, masters. Yet stand close.

BORACHIO
Therefore know I have earned of Don John a thousand ducats.

CONRADE
95 Is it possible that any villainy should be so dear?

BORACHIO
Thou shouldst rather ask if it were possible any villainy should be so rich. For when rich villains have need of poor ones, poor ones may make what price they will.

CONRADE
I wonder at it.

BORACHIO
100 That shows thou art unconfirmed. Thou knowest that the fashion of a doublet, or a hat, or a cloak, is nothing to a man.

CONRADE
Yes, it is apparel.

BORACHIO
I mean the fashion.

CONRADE
Yes, the fashion is the fashion.

BORACHIO

Come to think of it, I thought I felt a scab there.

CONRADE

I'll get you for that. Now get on with your story.

BORACHIO

Since it's drizzling, stand under this overhang with me and, like a true drunk, I'll tell you everything.

SEACOLE

(speaking so that only the other WATCHMEN *can hear)* There's some treason occurring, gentlemen. Stay here.

BORACHIO

You should know I've earned a thousand gold pieces from Don John.

CONRADE

Is it possible that any crime could be so valuable?

BORACHIO

You should ask instead if it's possible that any criminal could be so rich. Because when rich villains need poor villains' services, those poor ones can name the price.

CONRADE

I can't believe it.

BORACHIO

That only proves how inexperienced you are. You know that the style of a man's jacket or hat or coat means nothing.

CONRADE

Yes, it's just clothing.

BORACHIO

No, I mean, the fashion of a man's clothing tells us nothing about the man.

CONRADE

Yes, fashion is fashion.

BORACHIO

105   Tush, I may as well say the fool's the fool. But seest thou not
        what a deformed thief this fashion is?

SEACOLE

        (aside) I know that Deformed. He has been a vile thief this
        seven year. He goes up and down like a gentleman. I
        remember his name.

BORACHIO

110   Didst thou not hear somebody?

CONRADE

        No, 'twas the vane on the house.

BORACHIO

        Seest thou not, I say, what a deformed thief this fashion is,
        how giddily he turns about all the hot bloods between
        fourteen and five-and-thirty, sometimes fashioning them
115   like Pharaoh's soldiers in the reechy painting, sometime
        like god Bel's priests in the old church-window, sometime
        like the shaven Hercules in the smirched worm-eaten
        tapestry, where his codpiece seems as massy as his club?

CONRADE

        All this I see, and I see that the fashion wears out more
120   apparel than the man. But art not thou thyself giddy with
        the fashion too, that thou hast shifted out of thy tale into
        telling me of the fashion?

BORACHIO

        Not so, neither. But know that I have tonight wooed
        Margaret, the Lady Hero's gentlewoman, by the name of
125   Hero. She leans me out at her mistress' chamber window,
        bids me a thousand times good night. I tell this tale vilely.
        I should first tell thee how the Prince, Claudio and my
        master, planted and placed and possessed by my master
        Don John, saw afar off in the orchard this amiable
130   encounter.

BORACHIO

"Deformed" here means "deforming."

C'mon, I might as well say the fool's the fool! But don't you see what a deformed villain fashion is?

SEACOLE

The watchman thinks that "Deformed" is the name of one of the criminals.

(speaking so that only the other WATCHMEN *can hear)* I know that man, Deformed. For the past seven years, he's been a wicked thief. He walks around as if he were a gentleman. I remember that name.

BORACHIO

Did you hear someone?

CONRADE

Just the weathervane moving.

BORACHIO

A codpiece was a pouch, sometimes stuffed and decorated, worn over pants and covering a man's genitals.

As I was saying, fashion is a deformed villain. It makes hot-blooded young men spin around feverishly, forever changing their appearances, dictating that sometimes they dress like Pharoah's soldiers in that grimy painting and sometimes like the priests of the god Baal, as seen in old church windows. And sometimes fashion dresses them like the great Hercules in that dirty, worm-eaten tapestry—the one where his codpiece seems almost as big as his club.

CONRADE

I get all this. And I also understand how fashion changes so quickly that a man's clothing never gets a chance to wear itself out. But you're all wound up about fashion, too. Otherwise, why would you stray from your story to blabber on about it?

BORACHIO

No, I'm not wound up. But I will tell you that I seduced Margaret, the Lady Hero's waiting woman, tonight. I called her "Hero" the whole time. She leaned out of her mistress's bedroom window and told me good night a thousand times—but I am telling this story poorly. I should backtrack and begin with how my master, Don John, arranged for the Prince, Claudio, and himself to witness this friendly encounter from the orchard.

CONRADE
And thought they Margaret was Hero?

BORACHIO
Two of them did, the Prince and Claudio, but the devil my
master knew she was Margaret; and partly by his oaths,
which first possessed them, partly by the dark night, which
135   did deceive them, but chiefly by my villainy, which did
confirm any slander that Don John had made, away went
Claudio enraged, swore he would meet her as he was
appointed next morning at the temple, and there, before the
whole congregation, shame her with what he saw o'ernight
140   and send her home again without a husband.

FIRST WATCHMAN
We charge you, in the Prince's name, stand!

SEACOLE
Call up the right Master Constable. We have here
recovered the most dangerous piece of lechery that ever was
known in the commonwealth.

FIRST WATCHMAN
145   And one Deformed is one of them. I know him; he wears a
lock.

Exit FIRST WATCHMAN

CONRADE
Masters, masters—

SEACOLE
(to BORACHIO*)* You'll be made bring Deformed forth, I
warrant you.

CONRADE
150   Masters—

SEACOLE
Never speak: we charge you let us obey you to go with us.

CONRADE

And they thought Margaret was Hero?

BORACHIO

The Prince and Claudio did, but the devil, my master, knew that it was Margaret. They believed the charade partially because of my master's testimony—which first caused them to doubt Hero—and partially because of how dark and deceiving the night was, but mostly because of my villainous actions, which confirmed Don John's slander. Claudio went away enraged, swearing that he'd meet Hero at the temple as planned and there, before the entire congregation, shame her with what he'd discovered and send her home without a husband.

FIRST WATCHMAN

We charge you, in the Prince's name, to stop!

SEACOLE

Call up the Master Constable Dogberry. We have recovered the most dangerous piece of lechery that was ever known in the commonwealth.

recovered= discovered; lechery= treachery

FIRST WATCHMAN

And one of them is the criminal Deformed. I know him; he wears a lock of hair.

The **FIRST WATCHMAN** *exits.*

CONRADE

Gentlemen, gentlemen—

SEACOLE

(to **BORACHIO***)* I bet you'll be forced to bring Deformed forward.

CONRADE

Gentlemen—

SEACOLE

Don't speak. We obey you to go with us.

obey=order

BORACHIO
We are like to prove a goodly commodity, being taken up of
these men's bills.

CONRADE
A commodity in question, I warrant you.—Come, we'll
155 obey you.

Exeunt

BORACHIO

>We're probably a very valuable catch for these guys.

CONRADE

>Well, our value is debatable, I bet. Let's go, we'll obey
>you.

>*They all exit.*

ACT *3*, SCENE 4

Enter HERO, MARGARET, *and* URSULA

HERO
Good Ursula, wake my cousin Beatrice and desire her to rise.

URSULA
I will, lady.

HERO
And bid her come hither.

URSULA
5   Well.

Exit

MARGARET
Troth, I think your other rebato were better.

HERO
No, pray thee, good Meg, I'll wear this.

MARGARET
By my troth, 's not so good, and I warrant your cousin will say so.

HERO
10   My cousin's a fool, and thou art another. I'll wear none but this.

MARGARET
I like the new tire within excellently, if the hair were a thought browner; and your gown's a most rare fashion, i' faith. I saw the Duchess of Milan's gown that they praise so.

HERO
15   Oh, that exceeds, they say.

ACT 3, SCENE 4

HERO, MARGARET, *and* URSULA *enter.*

HERO

Good Ursula, go wake my cousin and ask her to get up.

URSULA

I will, lady.

HERO

And request that she come here.

URSULA

Very well.

She exits.

MARGARET

Really, I think your other ruff is better.

HERO

No, please good Meg, I'll wear this one.

MARGARET

Honestly, it's not as good as the other one, and I'm sure your cousin will agree with me.

HERO

My cousin's a fool, and you are too. I'll wear this one and none other.

MARGARET

I like your new wig and headdress, though I'd like it more if the hair were a shade browner. And your gown is really stylish. You know, I saw the Duchess of Milan's gown, the one that everyone praises so highly.

HERO

Oh, they say that dress surpasses all others.

MARGARET
By my troth, 's but a nightgown in respect of yours—cloth
o' gold, and cuts, and laced with silver, set with pearls,
down sleeves, side sleeves, and skirts, round underborne
with a bluish tinsel. But for a fine, quaint, graceful, and
20   excellent fashion, yours is worth ten on 't.

HERO
God give me joy to wear it, for my heart is exceeding heavy.

MARGARET
'Twill be heavier soon by the weight of a man.

HERO
Fie upon thee! Art not ashamed?

MARGARET
Of what, lady? Of speaking honorably? Is not marriage
25   honorable in a beggar? Is not your lord honorable without
marriage? I think you would have me say, "Saving your
reverence, a husband." An bad thinking do not wrest true
speaking, I'll offend nobody. Is there any harm in "the
heavier for a husband"? None, I think, an it be the right
30   husband and the right wife. Otherwise, 'tis light and not
heavy. Ask my Lady Beatrice else. Here she comes.

Enter **BEATRICE**

HERO
Good morrow, coz.

BEATRICE
Good morrow, sweet Hero.

MARGARET

Compared to your dress, it's no better than a night-gown. The cloth is interwoven with gold thread, and slashes in the material show the fabric beneath. It is trimmed with silver lace and embroidered with pearls. It has one set of fitted sleeves and another ornamental pair that hangs open from the shoulders. The skirts are trimmed with a blue, metallic fabric. But for a fine, elegant, graceful, and excellent dress, yours is worth ten of those.

HERO

I hope I enjoy wearing it, for my heart is very heavy.

MARGARET

It will be made even heavier soon—by the weight of a man.

HERO

Watch your tongue! Have you no shame?

MARGARET

Shame of what, lady? Sex and marriage are honorable things—even for a beggar, right? And isn't your husband an honorable man? You're so prudish you'd probably like me to say, "I beg your pardon, your *husband*"—as if husband were a dirty word! So long as suspicious minds aren't misinterpreting my honest words, I'll offend no one. What's wrong with admitting your husband's going to lie on you? Nothing, as long as it's the right husband with the right wife. That's right and proper—anything else is frivolous and immoral. Ask Beatrice. Here she comes.

BEATRICE *enters.*

HERO

Good morning, cousin.

BEATRICE

Good morning, sweet Hero.

HERO
Why, how now? Do you speak in the sick tune?

BEATRICE
35   I am out of all other tune, methinks.

MARGARET
Clap 's into "Light o' love." That goes without a burden.
Do you sing it, and I'll dance it.

BEATRICE
Ye light o' love, with your heels! Then, if your husband
have stables enough, you'll see he shall lack no barns.

MARGARET
40   O illegitimate construction! I scorn that with my heels.

BEATRICE
'Tis almost five o'clock, cousin. 'Tis time you were ready.
By my troth, I am exceeding ill. Heigh-ho!

MARGARET
For a hawk, a horse, or a husband?

BEATRICE
For the letter that begins them all, H.

MARGARET
45   Well, an you be not turned Turk, there's no more sailing by
the star.

BEATRICE
What means the fool, trow?

MARGARET
Nothing, I; but God send everyone their heart's desire.

HERO
These gloves the Count sent me, they are an excellent
50   perfume.

HERO

Why do you sound so odd? Are you ill? You sound out of tune.

BEATRICE

I must be ill—I don't think I can speak in any other tune.

MARGARET

If it's a tune we want, let's sing "Light on Love!" It's a light song and doesn't require a man to sing the baritone. You sing, and I'll dance.

BEATRICE

"Light-heeled" is slang for sexually loose.

You're "light on love" sure enough—your frivolous dancing proves you have light heels! When you're married one of these days, if your husband is rolling in dough, you'll let him roll in the hay whenever he wants.

MARGARET

Never! I reject that life; I kick it away with my heels.

BEATRICE

(to HERO*)* It's almost five o'clock, cousin. You should be ready by now. Oh, I really don't feel well. Heigh-ho!

MARGARET

Are you sighing for a hawk, a horse, or a husband?

BEATRICE

The word "ache" was once pronounced like the letter h.

I have an ache; I'm sighing for the letter that begins all those words.

MARGARET

Well, if you haven't renounced your old faith yet, we can't trust anything anymore.

BEATRICE

What does the fool mean by that, I wonder?

MARGARET

I don't mean anything—but God sends everyone their heart's desire.

HERO

The Count sent me an excellent pair of perfumed gloves.

BEATRICE

I am stuffed, cousin. I cannot smell.

MARGARET

A maid, and stuffed! There's goodly catching of cold.

BEATRICE

Oh, God help me, God help me! How long have you
professed apprehension?

MARGARET

55 Even since you left it. Doth not my wit become me rarely?

BEATRICE

It is not seen enough; you should wear it in your cap. By my
troth, I am sick.

MARGARET

Get you some of this distilled carduus benedictus and lay it
to your heart. It is the only thing for a qualm.

HERO

60 There thou prick'st her with a thistle.

BEATRICE

Benedictus! Why benedictus? You have some moral in this
benedictus?

MARGARET

Moral! No, by my troth, I have no moral meaning. I meant
plain holy thistle. You may think perchance that I think you
65 are in love. Nay, by 'r Lady, I am not such a fool to think
what I list, nor I list not to think what I can, nor indeed I
cannot think, if I would think my heart out of thinking, that
you are in love or that you will be in love or that you can be
in love. Yet Benedick was such another, and now is he
70 become a man. He swore he would never marry, and yet
now, in despite of his heart, he eats his meat without
grudging. And how you may be converted I know not, but
methinks you look with your eyes as other women do.

BEATRICE

Sorry, I'm all stuffed. I can't smell a thing.

MARGARET

Margaret makes an obscene pun on the word "stuffed."

Oh, just a young lady and already stuffed! That's a nice way to catch a cold.

BEATRICE

Oh, God help me! Since when have you claimed to be such a great wit?

MARGARET

Ever since you lost yours. Doesn't my wit suit me well?

BEATRICE

It doesn't get seen enough; you should wear it in your cap, the way fools wear coxcombs. God, I'm really sick.

MARGARET

carduus benedictus = "holy thistle," a medicinal herb good for the heart.

You should get some distilled *carduus benedictus* and put it on your chest. It's the only way to cure a sudden faintness.

HERO

With that you've managed to prick her with a thistle.

BEATRICE

Benedictus! Why do you suggest I use *benedictus*? Is there some double meaning in that word, "benedictus"?

MARGARET

Double meaning! No, honestly, there's no other meaning. I just meant that you should use some holy thistle. Maybe you think that I think you're in love. No, by Our Lady, I'm not such a fool to think what I please, and I don't please to think what I can, and in fact I cannot think, even if I could think my heart right past thinking, that you are in love or that you will be in love or even that you can be in love. But Benedick was once an enemy of love as well, and now he's become a real man. He swore that he'd never get married, but now, despite his earlier protestations, he loves ungrudgingly. How we're going to convert you I'll never know. And yet I think you look with your eyes just like every other woman does.

BEATRICE
What pace is this that thy tongue keeps?

MARGARET
75   Not a false gallop.

Enter URSULA

URSULA
Madam, withdraw: the Prince, the Count, Signor
Benedick, Don John, and all the gallants of the town are
come to fetch you to church.

HERO
Help to dress me, good coz, good Meg, good Ursula.

Exeunt

BEATRICE

Why are you talking at such a crazy clip?

MARGARET

It's not a false gallop, anyway.

URSULA enters.

URSULA

Madam, we have to go: the Prince, the Count, Signior Benedick, Don John, and all the gentlemen of the town have come to bring you to church.

HERO

Good cousin, good Meg, good Ursula, come help me get dressed.

They all exit.

ACT 3, SCENE 5

Enter LEONATO *with* DOGBERRY *and* VERGES

LEONATO
What would you with me, honest neighbor?

DOGBERRY
Marry, sir, I would have some confidence with you that
decerns you nearly.

LEONATO
Brief, I pray you, for you see it is a busy time with me.

DOGBERRY
5   Marry, this it is, sir.

VERGES
Yes, in truth it is, sir.

LEONATO
What is it, my good friends?

DOGBERRY
Goodman Verges, sir, speaks a little off the matter. An old
man, sir, and his wits are not so blunt as, God help, I would
10   desire they were, but, in faith, honest as the skin between
his brows.

VERGES
Yes, I thank God I am as honest as any man living that is an
old man and no honester than I.

DOGBERRY
Comparisons are odorous. *Palabras*, neighbor Verges.

LEONATO
15   Neighbors, you are tedious.

DOGBERRY
It pleases your Worship to say so, but we are the poor duke's
officers. But truly, for mine own part, if I were as tedious as
a king, I could find it in my heart to bestow it all of your
worship.

ACT 3. SCENE 5

LEONATO *enters with* DOGBERRY *and* VERGES.

LEONATO

What do you want from me, my good man?

DOGBERRY

"Decerns" is a mistake for "concerns."

Please, sir, I would like to discuss some news that decerns you greatly.

LEONATO

Be brief, please, because, as you can see, this is a busy time for me.

DOGBERRY

Indeed, sir, it is.

VERGES

Yes, it truly is.

LEONATO

What's the news, my good friends?

DOGBERRY

"Blunt" is a mistake for "sharp."

Sorry, sir, Goodman Verges tends to ramble. He's an old man, sir, and his wits are not as blunt as I wish they were. But truly, he's as honest as the skin between his brows.

VERGES

Yes, I thank God that I am as honest as all the other old men who are not honester than me.

DOGBERRY

"Odorous" is a mistake for "odious" (hateful).

Making comparisons is odorous, Verges. Get on with your story.

LEONATO

Friends, you are becoming tedious.

DOGBERRY

Dogberry takes "tedious" to mean "rich."

Thank you for saying that, your Worship, but we're just the poor duke's officers. But truly, if I were as tedious as a king, I would give everything to you, your Worship.

LEONATO

20   All thy tediousness on me, ah?

DOGBERRY

Yea, an 'twere a thousand pound more than 'tis, for I hear
as good exclamation on your Worship as of any man in the
city, and though I be but a poor man, I am glad to hear it.

VERGES

And so am I.

LEONATO

25   I would fain know what you have to say.

VERGES

Marry, sir, our watch tonight, excepting your Worship's
presence, ha' ta'en a couple of as arrant knaves as any in
Messina.

DOGBERRY

A good old man, sir. He will be talking. As they say, "When
30   the age is in, the wit is out." God help us, it is a world to see!
Well said, i' faith, neighbor Verges.—Well, God's a good
man. An two men ride of a horse, one must ride behind. An
honest soul, i' faith, sir, by my troth he is, as ever broke
bread, but God is to be worshipped, all men are not alike,
35   alas, good neighbor!

LEONATO

Indeed, neighbor, he comes too short of you.

DOGBERRY

Gifts that God gives.

LEONATO

I must leave you.

DOGBERRY

One word, sir. Our watch, sir, have indeed comprehended
40   two aspicious persons, and we would have them this
morning examined before your worship.

LEONATO

Oh, so you'd give me all your tediousness?

DOGBERRY

Yes, even if I had a thousand more pounds than that, for I hear that you are exclaimed throughout the city, and though I am only a poor man, it makes me glad to hear it.

"Exclaimed" is a mistake for "acclaimed."

VERGES

Me, too.

LEONATO

Gentlemen, please, I'd like to hear your news.

VERGES

"Expectfully" is a mistake for "respectfully."

Sir, our watch tonight—expectfully, sir—has captured a couple of the worst criminals in Messina.

DOGBERRY

(to LEONATO) Verges is a good old man, sir, but he's always babbling. Like they say, "When age comes, wit goes." God help us, what a world! *(to VERGES)* You did well, Verges, honestly. *(to LEONATO)* Well, God's a fair man. If two men are riding on one horse, one must naturally ride behind. Verges is as honest a man as any, but, God bless him, not all men are created equal. Am I right, my friend?

LEONATO

Truly, my friend, he isn't nearly as impressive as you are.

DOGBERRY

God gives those gifts—I had nothing to do with it.

LEONATO

Now I must return to the wedding.

DOGBERRY

One more thing, sir. Our watch, sir, as you know, has comprehended two auspicious persons. We'd like for you to examine them this morning.

"Comprehended" is a mistake for "apprehended"; "auspicious" is a mistake for "suspicious."

LEONATO
Take their examination yourself and bring it me. I am now
in great haste, as it may appear unto you.

DOGBERRY
It shall be suffigance.

LEONATO
45   Drink some wine ere you go. Fare you well.

Enter a MESSENGER

MESSENGER
My lord, they stay for you to give your daughter to her
husband.

LEONATO
I'll wait upon them. I am ready.

Exeunt LEONATO *and* MESSENGER

DOGBERRY
Go, good partner, go, get you to Francis Seacole. Bid him
50   bring his pen and inkhorn to the jail. We are now to
examination these men.

VERGES
And we must do it wisely.

DOGBERRY
We will spare for no wit, I warrant you. Here's that shall
drive some of them to a noncome. Only get the learned
55   writer to set down our excommunication and meet me at
the jail.

Exeunt

NO FEAR SHAKESPEARE

LEONATO

Examine them yourselves, then bring me your findings. Now I'm in a great hurry, as I'm sure you can see.

DOGBERRY

That will be suffigance. ◄──────

"Suffigance" is a mistake for "sufficient."

LEONATO

Have some wine before you go. Goodbye.

A MESSENGER *enters.*

MESSENGER

My lord, they're waiting for you to give your daughter away to Claudio.

LEONATO

I'm coming.

LEONATO *and the* MESSENGER *exit.*

DOGBERRY

"Examination" is a mistake for "examine."

Go to Francis Seacole, the constable of the watch. Tell him to bring his pen and his inkwell to the jail. We will now go to examination these men.

VERGES

We must do this wisely.

DOGBERRY

"Noncome" is a mistake for "outcome"; "excommunication" is a mistake for "examination."

We won't hold back any of our wisdom. We'll drive them to a noncome. Go get the educated writer to record our excommunication, and I'll meet you at the jail.

They all exit.

ACT FOUR
SCENE 1

Enter DON PEDRO, DON JOHN, LEONATO, FRIAR FRANCIS, CLAUDIO, BENEDICK, HERO, BEATRICE, *and Attendants*

LEONATO
Come, Friar Francis, be brief, only to the plain form of marriage, and you shall recount their particular duties afterwards.

FRIAR FRANCIS
(to CLAUDIO*)* You come hither, my lord, to marry this lady?

CLAUDIO
5   No.

LEONATO
To be married to her.—Friar, you come to marry her.

FRIAR FRANCIS
Lady, you come hither to be married to this count?

HERO
I do.

FRIAR FRANCIS
If either of you know any inward impediment why you
10   should not be conjoined, charge you on your souls to utter it.

CLAUDIO
Know you any, Hero?

HERO
None, my lord.

FRIAR FRANCIS
Know you any, count?

ACT FOUR
SCENE 1

DON PEDRO, DON JOHN, LEONATO, FRIAR FRANCIS,
CLAUDIO, BENEDICK, HERO, *and* BEATRICE *enter with*
ATTENDANTS.

LEONATO

> All right, Friar Francis, let's keep this short. Do a sim-
> ple ceremony, and list all the particular duties of mar-
> riage later.

FRIAR FRANCIS

> *(to* CLAUDIO*)* Have you come here, my lord, to marry
> this lady?

CLAUDIO

> No.

LEONATO

> No, he comes to be married *to* her. Friar, you are the
> one who has come to marry her.

FRIAR FRANCIS

> Lady, do you come here to be married to this count?

HERO

> I do.

FRIAR FRANCIS

> If either of you knows any secret reason why you two
> should not be joined in marriage, I order you on your
> souls to say so.

CLAUDIO

> Do you know any, Hero?

HERO

> None, my lord.

FRIAR FRANCIS

> Do you know any, count?

LEONATO

15   I dare make his answer, none.

CLAUDIO

O, what men dare do! What men may do! What men daily
do, not knowing what they do!

BENEDICK

How now, interjections? Why, then, some be of laughing,
as, ah, ha, he!

CLAUDIO

20   Stand thee by, Friar.—Father, by your leave,
Will you with free and unconstrainèd soul
Give me this maid, your daughter?

LEONATO

As freely, son, as God did give her me.

CLAUDIO

And what have I to give you back whose worth
25   May counterpoise this rich and precious gift?

DON PEDRO

Nothing, unless you render her again.

CLAUDIO

Sweet Prince, you learn me noble thankfulness.—
There, Leonato, take her back again.
Give not this rotten orange to your friend.
30   She's but the sign and semblance of her honor.
Behold how like a maid she blushes here!
Oh, what authority and show of truth
Can cunning sin cover itself withal!
Comes not that blood as modest evidence
35   To witness simple virtue? Would you not swear,
All you that see her, that she were a maid
By these exterior shows? But she is none.
She knows the heat of a luxurious bed.
Her blush is guiltiness, not modesty.

LEONATO

I'm sure I can answer for him—he doesn't know any, either.

CLAUDIO

Oh, the things men dare to do! The things men are allowed to do! The things men do daily, not knowing what they're doing!

BENEDICK

Benedick is jokingly referring to a passage from a popular Latin grammar book of the day.

What, are we playing with interjections? Well then, add some interjections that indicate laughter, like "ah," "ha," and "he!"

CLAUDIO

Hold on, Friar. *(to* LEONATO*)* Father, are you giving me your daughter freely?

LEONATO

As freely, son, as God gave her to me.

CLAUDIO

And what should I give you that would be equal in value to this rare and precious gift?

DON PEDRO

Nothing, sir, except grandchildren.

CLAUDIO

Good Prince, you have taught me how to accept things nobly. There, Leonato, take your daughter back. Don't insult a friend by giving him a beautiful orange that rots inside. She only appears honorable from the outside. Look, how she blushes like a virgin! Oh, sin can disguise itself so artfully! Doesn't that rising blush suggest that she is virtuous and innocent? All of you who are looking at her, wouldn't you swear that she's a virgin, judging by these outward shows? But she is no virgin. She has been in a man's bed. She blushes from guilt, not modesty.

LEONATO
40   What do you mean, my lord?

CLAUDIO
                                        Not to be married,
        Not to knit my soul to an approvèd wanton.

LEONATO
        Dear my lord, if you in your own proof
        Have vanquished the resistance of her youth
        And made defeat of her virginity—

CLAUDIO
45   I know what you would say: if I have known her,
        You will say she did embrace me as a husband,
        And so extenuate the forehand sin.
        No, Leonato,
        I never tempted her with word too large
50   But, as a brother to his sister, showed
        Bashful sincerity and comely love.

HERO
        And seemed I ever otherwise to you?

CLAUDIO
        Out on thee, seeming! I will write against it.
        You seem to me as Dian in her orb,
55   As chaste as is the bud ere it be blown.
        But you are more intemperate in your blood
        Than Venus, or those pampered animals
        That rage in savage sensuality.

HERO
        Is my lord well, that he doth speak so wide?

LEONATO
60   Sweet Prince, why speak not you?

DON PEDRO
                                        What should I speak?
        I stand dishonored, that have gone about
        To link my dear friend to a common stale.

LEONATO
        Are these things spoken, or do I but dream?

LEONATO

What do you mean, my lord?

CLAUDIO

I won't be married. I won't join my soul to such a proven slut.

LEONATO

My dear lord, if it was you who conquered her and took her virginity—

CLAUDIO

I know what you're about to say. If I had slept with her, you'd say that we did so as husband and wife, merely anticipating our eventual marriage. No, Leonato. I never seduced her, or tempted her with indecent words. I treated her like a brother would treat a sister, with modest sincerity and appropriate affection.

HERO

And have I ever seemed less than modest or appropriate to you?

CLAUDIO

Diana was the virgin goddess of the hunt and moon; Venus was the goddess of love, generally portrayed as fickle and promiscuous.

Curse you for your false appearances! To me, you seemed like Diana in her orbit—as virginal as the flower bud before it blooms. But you're actually as hot-blooded as Venus, or a pampered animal allowed to run wild.

HERO

Are you sick, my lord? Is that why you're talking so wildly?

LEONATO

Good Prince, say something!

DON PEDRO

What should I say? I've been dishonored: I arranged for a friend of mine to marry a common whore.

LEONATO

Are you really saying these things, or am I dreaming?

DON JOHN
Sir, they are spoken, and these things are true.

BENEDICK
65   This looks not like a nuptial.

HERO
True! O God!

CLAUDIO
Leonato, stand I here?
Is this the Prince? Is this the Prince's brother?
Is this face Hero's? Are our eyes our own?

LEONATO
70   All this is so, but what of this, my lord?

CLAUDIO
Let me but move one question to your daughter,
And by that fatherly and kindly power
That you have in her, bid her answer truly.

LEONATO
I charge thee do so, as thou art my child.

HERO
75   Oh, God defend me! how am I beset!—
What kind of catechizing call you this?

CLAUDIO
To make you answer truly to your name.

HERO
Is it not Hero? Who can blot that name
With any just reproach?

CLAUDIO
Marry, that can Hero!
80   Hero itself can blot out Hero's virtue.
What man was he talked with you yesternight
Out at your window betwixt twelve and one?
Now, if you are a maid, answer to this.

HERO
I talked with no man at that hour, my lord.

DON JOHN

They're really being spoken, sir, and they're true.

BENEDICK

This doesn't look like a wedding.

HERO

It's true! Oh God!

CLAUDIO

Leonato, am I standing here? Is this the Prince? Is this the Prince's brother? Is this face Hero's? Are these our eyes?

LEONATO

Yes, that's all true—but what do you mean by it, my lord?

CLAUDIO

Let me just ask her one question, and by your authority as her father, order her to answer truthfully.

LEONATO

As my child, I order you to do so.

HERO

Oh, God help me! How I'm being attacked! What kind of game is this?

CLAUDIO

We just want you to answer to your real name.

HERO

Isn't my name Hero? Who can stain that name with a just accusation?

CLAUDIO

Indeed, Hero herself can! You've stained your virtue with your own actions. What man were you talking to at your window last night, between the hours of midnight and one? If you're a virgin, you'll answer this question.

HERO

I wasn't talking to any man at that time, my lord.

DON PEDRO

85   Why, then are you no maiden.—Leonato,
      I am sorry you must hear. Upon mine honor,
      Myself, my brother, and this grievèd count
      Did see her, hear her, at that hour last night
      Talk with a ruffian at her chamber window
90   Who hath indeed, most like a liberal villain,
      Confessed the vile encounters they have had
      A thousand times in secret.

DON JOHN

      Fie, fie, they are not to be named, my lord,
      Not to be spoke of!
95   There is not chastity enough in language,
      Without offense, to utter them.—Thus, pretty lady,
      I am sorry for thy much misgovernment.

CLAUDIO

      O Hero, what a Hero hadst thou been
      If half thy outward graces had been placed
100   About thy thoughts and counsels of thy heart!
      But fare thee well, most foul, most fair! Farewell,
      Thou pure impiety and impious purity.
      For thee I'll lock up all the gates of love,
      And on my eyelids shall conjecture hang,
105   To turn all beauty into thoughts of harm,
      And never shall it more be gracious.

LEONATO

      Hath no man's dagger here a point for me?

HERO *swoons*

BEATRICE

      Why, how now, cousin! wherefore sink you down?

DON JOHN

      Come, let us go. These things, come thus to light,
110   Smother her spirits up.

                    Exeunt **DON PEDRO**, **DON JOHN**, *and* **CLAUDIO**

DON PEDRO

Well then, you are no virgin. Leonato, I'm sorry you have to hear this. I swear on my honor that we saw and heard Hero talking to a brute at her window last night. And that man confessed at length how he has secretly come to her bedroom thousands of times.

DON JOHN

No, my lord, don't name her sinful acts or speak of them! There's no way to describe them without offending everyone here. Pretty lady, I'm much ashamed of your shocking behavior.

CLAUDIO

The mythical Hero, who died for her lover, Leander, was considered the model of perfect love.

Oh Hero, you could have equaled the mythical Hero if only half your outward beauty matched your inner thoughts and desires! Goodbye, beautiful sinner. Goodbye to your pure wickedness and your wicked purity. Because of you, I'll keep myself away from love. I'll hang suspicion on my eyelids, so that all the beautiful things I see are transformed into dangers and are never able to trick me again.

LEONATO

Does anyone have a dagger for me?

HERO *faints.*

BEATRICE

What's wrong, cousin? Why have you collapsed?

DON JOHN

Come, let's go. These revelations have overwhelmed her.

DON PEDRO, **DON JOHN**, *and* **CLAUDIO** *exit.*

BENEDICK
How doth the lady?

BEATRICE
                    Dead, I think.—Help, uncle!—
Hero, why, Hero! Uncle! Signor Benedick! Friar!

LEONATO
O Fate! Take not away thy heavy hand!
Death is the fairest cover for her shame
115 That may be wished for.

BEATRICE
How now, cousin Hero!

HERO *stirs*

FRIAR FRANCIS
(to HERO*)* Have comfort, lady.

LEONATO
(to HERO*)* Dost thou look up?

FRIAR FRANCIS
                    Yea, wherefore should she not?

LEONATO
Wherefore! Why, doth not every earthly thing
120 Cry shame upon her? Could she here deny
The story that is printed in her blood?—
Do not live, Hero, do not ope thine eyes,
For, did I think thou wouldst not quickly die,
Thought I thy spirits were stronger than thy shames,
125 Myself would, on the rearward of reproaches,
Strike at thy life. Grieved I I had but one?
Chid I for that at frugal Nature's frame?
O, one too much by thee! Why had I one?
Why ever wast thou lovely in my eyes?
130 Why had I not with charitable hand
Took up a beggar's issue at my gates,
Who, smirchèd thus, and mired with infamy,
I might have said, "No part of it is mine;
This shame derives itself from unknown loins"?

BENEDICK

How is she?

BEATRICE

She's dead, I think.—Help, uncle!—Hero, why Hero! Uncle! Signior Benedick! Friar!

LEONATO

Oh Fate, don't spare Hero from being punished! Death is the best way to cover over her shame.

BEATRICE

How are you, Hero?

HERO stirs.

FRIAR FRANCIS

(to HERO) Take comfort, lady.

LEONATO

(to HERO) Are you looking up?

FRIAR FRANCIS

Yes, why shouldn't she?

LEONATO

Why not! Isn't every living thing condemning her? Can she deny the accusations that are proven by her guilty blush? Die, Hero, don't open your eyes. If I didn't think you were about to die soon—if I thought your spirit could bear this shame—I would risk punishment and kill you myself. Am I sorry that I only had one child? Do I blame Nature for being so thrifty? Oh, one child is one too many! Why did I ever have one? Why did you once seem lovely to me? Why didn't I just adopt a beggar's child left at my doorstep, whose shame and dishonor I could have denied, not being its true father?

135 But mine, and mine I loved, and mine I praised,
And mine that I was proud on, mine so much
That I myself was to myself not mine,
Valuing of her—why, she, O she is fall'n
Into a pit of ink, that the wide sea
140 Hath drops too few to wash her clean again
And salt too little which may season give
To her foul tainted flesh!

BENEDICK
                                        Sir, sir, be patient.
For my part, I am so attired in wonder
I know not what to say.

BEATRICE
145 Oh, on my soul, my cousin is belied!

BENEDICK
Lady, were you her bedfellow last night?

BEATRICE
No, truly not, although until last night
I have this twelvemonth been her bedfellow.

LEONATO
Confirmed, confirmed! Oh, that is stronger made
150 Which was before barred up with ribs of iron!
Would the two princes lie and Claudio lie,
Who loved her so that, speaking of her foulness,
Washed it with tears? Hence from her. Let her die.

FRIAR FRANCIS
Hear me a little,
155 For I have only silent been so long,
And given way unto this course of fortune,
By noting of the lady. I have marked
A thousand blushing apparitions
To start into her face, a thousand innocent shames
160 In angel whiteness beat away those blushes,
And in her eye there hath appeared a fire
To burn the errors that these princes hold
Against her maiden truth. Call me a fool,

But you were mine, and I loved and praised you for being mine, and was proud of you for being mine—I loved you so much that I hardly cared about myself. Oh, but now you have fallen into a pit of ink, and there's not enough water in the whole wide sea to wash you clean again, and not enough salt to cover your stink.

BENEDICK

Sir, sir, calm down. I'm so amazed by this, I don't know what to say.

BEATRICE

Oh, on my soul, my cousin has been slandered falsely!

BENEDICK

Lady, did you sleep in her room last night?

BEATRICE

No, I didn't, but I did every night for the past year.

LEONATO

Then it's confirmed! That's even more proof, and the case against her was airtight already. Would the two princes and Claudio lie? Claudio, who loved her so much that talking about her wickedness made him weep?

FRIAR FRANCIS

Listen to me a moment. I've only remained silent this whole time because I've been watching Hero. I've seen her begin to blush a thousand times, only to watch those blushes disappear a thousand times and an innocent paleness take over her face. And in her eyes I see a fire that would seem to burn away the lies the princes have told about her chastity. Call me a fool,

Trust not my reading nor my observations,
165   Which with experimental seal doth warrant
The tenor of my book; trust not my age,
My reverence, calling, nor divinity,
If this sweet lady lie not guiltless here
Under some biting error.

LEONATO

                      Friar, it cannot be.
170   Thou seest that all the grace that she hath left
Is that she will not add to her damnation
A sin of perjury. She not denies it.
Why seek'st thou then to cover with excuse
That which appears in proper nakedness?

FRIAR FRANCIS

175   Lady, what man is he you are accused of?

HERO

They know that do accuse me. I know none.
If I know more of any man alive
Than that which maiden modesty doth warrant,
Let all my sins lack mercy!—O my father,
180   Prove you that any man with me conversed
At hours unmeet, or that I yesternight
Maintained the change of words with any creature,
Refuse me, hate me, torture me to death!

FRIAR FRANCIS

There is some strange misprision in the princes.

BENEDICK

185   Two of them have the very bent of honor,
And if their wisdoms be misled in this,
The practice of it lives in John the Bastard,
Whose spirits toil in frame of villainies.

don't trust my observations—the truth of which is backed up by all my years of experience—don't trust my age, my reputation, my position, and my holiness. You can doubt all these things if this sweet lady turns out to be guilty.

LEONATO

But she must be, Friar. You see that any morals she has left are preventing her from denying the charges: she doesn't want to add perjury to her list of sins.

FRIAR FRANCIS

Lady, who do they accuse you of having taken as your lover?

HERO

You should ask them. I don't know who they're talking about. If I've been with a man in any improper way, let all my sins be punished! Oh, father, if you yourself can prove that I talked with a man at an indecent hour, or indeed that I spoke to any creature last night, you can disown me, hate me, and torture me to death!

FRIAR FRANCIS

The princes are under some strange misunderstanding.

BENEDICK

Two of them are completely honorable, and if they have been tricked in this, we must blame John the Bastard, who lives to create conflict.

LEONATO

I know not. If they speak but truth of her,

190 These hands shall tear her; if they wrong her honor,

The proudest of them shall well hear of it.

Time hath not yet so dried this blood of mine

Nor age so eat up my invention

Nor fortune made such havoc of my means

195 Nor my bad life reft me so much of friends

But they shall find, awaked in such a kind,

Both strength of limb and policy of mind,

Ability in means and choice of friends,

To quit me of them throughly.

FRIAR FRANCIS

Pause awhile,

200 And let my counsel sway you in this case.

Your daughter here the princes left for dead.

Let her awhile be secretly kept in

And publish it that she is dead indeed.

Maintain a mourning ostentation,

205 And on your family's old monument

Hang mournful epitaphs and do all rites

That appertain unto a burial.

LEONATO

What shall become of this? What will this do?

FRIAR FRANCIS

Marry, this, well carried, shall on her behalf

210 Change slander to remorse. That is some good.

But not for that dream I on this strange course,

But on this travail look for greater birth.

She, dying, as it must so be maintained,

Upon the instant that she was accused,

215 Shall be lamented, pitied and excused

Of every hearer. For it so falls out

That what we have we prize not to the worth

Whiles we enjoy it, but being lacked and lost,

Why then we rack the value, then we find

LEONATO

I don't know. If they have spoken the truth about Hero, I will tear her apart with my bare hands. But if they have accused her falsely, even the greatest of them will have to deal with me. Age hasn't dried up my body or eroded my intelligence so much, and luck hasn't robbed me of so much of my fortune, and my bad ways haven't deprived me of so many friends, that they won't find me ready to seek revenge both physically and mentally, with money and friends at my disposal.

FRIAR FRANCIS

Hold on a moment, and listen to my advice. The princes left your daughter here for dead. Hide her for a while in your house, and tell everyone that she has, in fact, died. Make a bug show of mourning for her, hang sad epitaphs up at your family's tomb, and perform all the appropriate burial ceremonies.

LEONATO

Why should we do this? What will this do?

FRIAR FRANCIS

Listen, if we do this correctly, the men who slandered Hero will feel remorse for her instead. That will be a good thing. But I have an even greater goal in mind. We'll maintain that she died the instant she was accused, and everyone who hears this will grieve for her, pity her, and excuse her actions. That's how it goes: we don't value the things we have until we lose them, when we suddenly rack up their value and see

220   The virtue that possession would not show us
        Whiles it was ours. So will it fare with Claudio.
        When he shall hear she died upon his words,
        The idea of her life shall sweetly creep
        Into his study of imagination,
225   And every lovely organ of her life
        Shall come apparelled in more precious habit,
        More moving, delicate and full of life,
        Into the eye and prospect of his soul
        Than when she lived indeed. Then shall he mourn,
230   If ever love had interest in his liver,
        And wish he had not so accused her,
        No, though he thought his accusation true.
        Let this be so, and doubt not but success
        Will fashion the event in better shape
235   Than I can lay it down in likelihood.
        But if all aim but this be leveled false,
        The supposition of the lady's death
        Will quench the wonder of her infamy.
        And if it sort not well, you may conceal her,
240   As best befits her wounded reputation,
        In some reclusive and religious life,
        Out of all eyes, tongues, minds, and injuries.

BENEDICK
        Signior Leonato, let the friar advise you.
        And though you know my inwardness and love
245   Is very much unto the Prince and Claudio,
        Yet, by mine honor, I will deal in this
        As secretly and justly as your soul
        Should with your body.

LEONATO
                                Being that I flow in grief,
        The smallest twine may lead me.

all the virtues we were blind to when they were alive and with us. That's how Claudio will respond. When he hears that she died from his words, his imagination will be sweetly overtaken by thoughts of her. In death, every aspect of her life will be got up more beautifully, and in his mind she will seem more moving, more delicate, and more lively even than when she was alive. Then, if he ever truly felt love, he'll mourn and wish he hadn't accused her—even though he believed his accusation to be true. Follow my plan, and trust that the actual events will play out even better than I am describing. And even if they don't, at least Hero's supposed death will stop the rumors of her infidelity. And if it doesn't go well, then you can keep her hidden in a nunnery, the best place for someone with her kind of dirtied reputation—away from the public's eyes, tongues, mind, and insults.

BENEDICK

Signior Leonato, listen to the friar's plan. And even though you know I'm very close to the Prince and Claudio, I swear I'll keep your counsel and deal with this secretly and justly.

LEONATO

Because I'm drowning in my grief, I'll grab onto the smallest piece of string dangled in front of me.

FRIAR FRANCIS
250   'Tis well consented. Presently away,
        For to strange sores strangely they strain the cure.—
        Come, lady, die to live. This wedding day
        Perhaps is but prolonged. Have patience and endure.

                              Exeunt all but BENEDICK *and* BEATRICE

BENEDICK
        Lady Beatrice, have you wept all this while?

BEATRICE
255   Yea, and I will weep a while longer.

BENEDICK
        I will not desire that.

BEATRICE
        You have no reason. I do it freely.

BENEDICK
        Surely I do believe your fair cousin is wronged.

BEATRICE
        Ah, how much might the man deserve of me that would
260   right her!

BENEDICK
        Is there any way to show such friendship?

BEATRICE
        A very even way, but no such friend.

BENEDICK
        May a man do it?

BEATRICE
        It is a man's office, but not yours.

BENEDICK
265   I do love nothing in the world so well as you. Is not that
        strange?

BEATRICE
        As strange as the thing I know not. It were as possible for
        me to say I loved nothing so well as you, but believe me not,
        and yet I lie not, I confess nothing, nor I deny nothing. I am
270   sorry for my cousin.

FRIAR FRANCIS

This is a good agreement. Now, let's go. A strange disease requires a strange cure. Come, lady; you must die in order to live. Hopefully, your wedding day is only postponed. Have patience and endure.

Everyone but BENEDICK *and* BEATRICE *exits.*

BENEDICK

Lady Beatrice, have you been crying this entire time?

BEATRICE

Yes, and I'll keep crying a while longer.

BENEDICK

I don't wish that on you.

BEATRICE

You don't have to; I do it of my own free will.

BENEDICK

I really believe your cousin was falsely accused.

BEATRICE

Oh, the man who avenged her could ask anything of me!

BENEDICK

Is there any way I could show such friendship to you?

BEATRICE

A very clear way, but there is no friend who will undertake it.

BENEDICK

Can a man do it?

BEATRICE

It's a job meant for a man, but not you.

BENEDICK

There is nothing in the world that I love as much as you. Isn't that strange?

BEATRICE

It's as strange as this other thing which I don't understand. I could just as easily say that there is nothing in the world that I love as much as you. But don't believe me—though I'm not lying. I confess nothing, and I deny nothing. I feel awful for my cousin.

BENEDICK
By my sword, Beatrice, thou lovest me.

BEATRICE
Do not swear, and eat it.

BENEDICK
I will swear by it that you love me, and I will make him eat
it that says I love not you.

BEATRICE
275   Will you not eat your word?

BENEDICK
With no sauce that can be devised to it. I protest I love thee.

BEATRICE
Why then, God forgive me.

BENEDICK
What offense, sweet Beatrice?

BEATRICE
You have stayed me in a happy hour. I was about to protest
280   I loved you.

BENEDICK
And do it with all thy heart.

BEATRICE
I love you with so much of my heart that none is left to
protest.

BENEDICK
Come, bid me do anything for thee.

BEATRICE
285   Kill Claudio.

BENEDICK
Ha! Not for the wide world.

BEATRICE
You kill me to deny it. Farewell.

BEATRICE *begins to exit*

BENEDICK

By my sword, Beatrice, you love me.

BEATRICE

Beatrice means "eat your words" (i.e., go back on your pledge to love me)…

Don't swear like that and then go back and eat it later.

BENEDICK

…but Benedick takes it to mean "eat your sword."

I'll swear by my sword that you love me, too, and I'll make any man who says that I don't love you eat it.

BEATRICE

But you won't eat your words?

BENEDICK

Not with any sauce they could provide for them. I swear, I love you.

BEATRICE

Well then, God forgive me!

BENEDICK

Why, what have you done, sweet Beatrice?

BEATRICE

You got to me first. I was about to swear that I loved you.

BENEDICK

Then do so, with all your heart.

BEATRICE

I love you with so much of my heart that none of it is left to protest with.

BENEDICK

Come, ask me to do anything for you.

BEATRICE

Kill Claudio.

BENEDICK

Ha! I wouldn't do that for the whole wide world.

BEATRICE

Then, rejecting my request, you kill *me*, instead. Goodbye.

BEATRICE *begins to exit.*

BENEDICK
Tarry, sweet Beatrice.

BEATRICE
I am gone, though I am here. There is no love in you. Nay,
290   I pray you let me go.

BENEDICK
Beatrice—

BEATRICE
In faith, I will go.

BENEDICK
We'll be friends first.

BEATRICE
You dare easier be friends with me than fight with mine
295   enemy.

BENEDICK
Is Claudio thine enemy?

BEATRICE
Is he not approved in the height a villain, that hath
slandered, scorned, dishonored my kinswoman? Oh, that I
were a man! What, bear her in hand until they come to take
300   hands and then, with public accusation, uncovered
slander, unmitigated rancor—O God, that I were a man! I
would eat his heart in the marketplace.

BENEDICK
Hear me, Beatrice—

BEATRICE
Talk with a man out at a window! A proper saying!

BENEDICK
305   Nay, but Beatrice—

BEATRICE
Sweet Hero, she is wronged, she is slandered, she is
undone.

BENEDICK
Beat—

BENEDICK

Wait, sweet Beatrice.

BEATRICE

My body waits here, but the rest of me is gone. You don't really love me. I beg you to let me go.

BENEDICK

Beatrice—

BEATRICE

I swear, I'm going.

BENEDICK

Not until we part as friends.

BEATRICE

How dare you try to be my friend when you refuse to fight my enemy.

BENEDICK

Is Claudio your enemy?

BEATRICE

Hasn't he proven himself to be a great villain—slandering, scorning, and dishonoring my cousin? Oh, I wish I were a man! He pretended that everything was fine until the moment they were exchanging vows, and then—with public accusation, blatant slander, pure hatred—Oh God, if only I were a man! I would rip his heart out in public and eat it.

BENEDICK

Listen to me, Beatrice—

BEATRICE

Talking with a man outside her bedroom window! A likely story!

BENEDICK

No, but Beatrice—

BEATRICE

Sweet Hero, she's been wronged, she's been slandered, she's been ruined.

BENEDICK

Beat—

BEATRICE
Princes and counties! Surely, a princely testimony, a goodly
310 count, Count Comfect, a sweet gallant, surely! Oh, that I
were a man for his sake! Or that I had any friend would be
a man for my sake! But manhood is melted into curtsies,
valor into compliment, and men are only turned into
tongue, and trim ones too. He is now as valiant as Hercules
315 that only tells a lie and swears it. I cannot be a man with
wishing, therefore I will die a woman with grieving.

BENEDICK
Tarry, good Beatrice. By this hand, I love thee.

BEATRICE
Use it for my love some other way than swearing by it.

BENEDICK
Think you in your soul the Count Claudio hath wronged
320 Hero?

BEATRICE
Yea, as sure as I have a thought or a soul.

BENEDICK
Enough, I am engaged. I will challenge him. I will kiss your
hand, and so I leave you. By this hand, Claudio shall render
me a dear account. As you hear of me, so think of me. Go
325 comfort your cousin. I must say she is dead, and so,
farewell.

Exeunt

BEATRICE

Princes and counts! Oh, of course, it was all so proper and ceremonious—they gave a truly princely testimony. He's a proper count, that Count Sugarplum, a sweet gentleman, for sure! Oh, if only I were a man! Or had a friend who would be a man for me! But there are no real men left. Their manliness has melted into pretty curtsies and fancy manners, and their bravery is spent on making clever compliments. All this conversing has turned men into tongues—and fancy ones, at that. The man who tells a lie and swears by it is now considered as brave as Hercules. I can't make myself a man by wishing I were, so as a woman I'll die, from grieving.

Hercules was a great hero in Greek and Roman mythology.

BENEDICK

Wait, good Beatrice. I swear by this hand that I love you.

BEATRICE

Don't just swear by it; put your hand to some use that will prove you love me.

BENEDICK

Do you honestly think, in your soul, that Claudio has wrongly accused Hero?

BEATRICE

Yes, as sure as I have a thought or a soul.

BENEDICK

That's enough for me, then. I'll challenge him. I'll kiss your hand, and with that I leave you. I swear that Claudio will pay dearly for this. Keep me in your thoughts and go comfort your cousin. I'll go tell them that she's dead. Goodbye.

They exit.

ACT 4, SCENE 2

Enter DOGBERRY, VERGES, *and* SEXTON, *in gowns; and the*
Watch, with CONRADE *and* BORACHIO

DOGBERRY
Is our whole dissembly appeared?

VERGES
Oh, a stool and a cushion for the Sexton.

A stool is brought in. SEXTON *sits*

SEXTON
Which be the malefactors?

DOGBERRY
Marry, that am I and my partner.

VERGES
5   Nay, that's certain; we have the exhibition to examine.

SEXTON
But which are the offenders that are to be examined? Let
them come before Master Constable.

DOGBERRY
Yea, marry, let them come before me.
What is your name, friend?

BORACHIO *and* CONRADE *come forward*

BORACHIO
10   Borachio.

DOGBERRY
Pray, write down, "Borachio."—Yours, sirrah?

CONRADE
I am a gentleman, sir, and my name is Conrade.

ACT 4, SCENE 2

DOGBERRY, VERGES, *the* SEXTON *(in his official gown), and the* WATCHMEN *enter, bringing* CONRADE *and* BORACHIO.

DOGBERRY

Is our whole dissembly here? ←——

"Dissembly" is a mistake for "assembly."

VERGES

Oh, we need a stool and a cushion for the sexton.

A stool is brought in. The SEXTON *sits down.*

SEXTON

Which ones are the malefactors?

DOGBERRY

Sir, that would be me and my partner.

VERGES

"Exhibitioned" is a mistake for "commissioned."

Yes, yes, we've been exhibitioned to examine this case.

SEXTON

No, you've misunderstood me—where are the criminals whom I'm supposed to examine? Have them come in front of the master constable.

DOGBERRY

Yes, indeed, bring them before me.

BORACHIO *and* CONRADE *come forward.*

What's your name, friend?

BORACHIO

Borachio.

DOGBERRY

Please, write down "Borachio."—And yours?

CONRADE

I'm a gentleman, sir, and my name is Conrade.

DOGBERRY
Write down "Master Gentleman Conrade."—Masters, do you serve God?

CONRADE, BORACHIO
15   Yea, sir, we hope.

DOGBERRY
Write down that they hope they serve God; and write God first, for God defend but God should go before such villains!—Masters, it is proved already that you are little better than false knaves, and it will go near to be thought so
20   shortly. How answer you for yourselves?

CONRADE
Marry, sir, we say we are none.

DOGBERRY
A marvelous witty fellow, I assure you, but I will go about with him.—Come you hither, sirrah, a word in your ear. Sir, I say to you it is thought you are false knaves.

BORACHIO
25   Sir, I say to you we are none.

DOGBERRY
Well, stand aside.—'Fore God, they are both in a tale. Have you writ down that they are none?

SEXTON
Master Constable, you go not the way to examine. You must call forth the watch that are their accusers.

DOGBERRY
30   Yea, marry, that's the eftest way.—Let the watch come forth. Masters, I charge you in the Prince's name, accuse these men.

DOGBERRY

Write down "Master Gentleman Conrade."—Gentlemen, are you good Christians, and do you serve God?

CONRADE, BORACHIO

Yes, sir, we hope so.

DOGBERRY

Write down that they hope they serve God. Oh, and write "God" first—for God forbid we put these criminals before God!—Gentlemen, it's already been proven that you aren't much better than lying criminals, and soon we'll know almost for certain. How do you both plead?

CONRADE

Honestly, sir, we say that we are not criminals.

DOGBERRY

He's a marvelously witty fellow, no doubt, but I'll outmaneuver him.—Come over here; I'll whisper a word in your ear. Sir, I tell you we believe you're both lying criminals.

BORACHIO

Sir, I tell you that we are not.

DOGBERRY

Well, okay.—I swear to God, both their stories match. Have you written that down, that they aren't criminals?

SEXTON

Master Constable, you're going about this all wrong. First, you have to speak to the watchmen who accused them.

DOGBERRY

"Eftest" is a mistake for "aptest."

Yes, good idea; that's the eftest way. Bring the watchmen forward. Gentlemen, I order you in the Prince's name to accuse these men.

FIRST WATCHMAN
This man said, sir, that Don John, the Prince's brother, was
a villain.

DOGBERRY
35   Write down Prince John a villain. Why, this is flat perjury,
to call a prince's brother villain.

BORACHIO
Master Constable—

DOGBERRY
Pray thee, fellow, peace. I do not like thy look, I promise
thee.

SEXTON
40   *(to Watch)* What heard you him say else?

SECOND WATCHMAN
Marry, that he had received a thousand ducats of Don John
for accusing the Lady Hero wrongfully.

DOGBERRY
Flat burglary as ever was committed.

VERGES
Yea, by Mass, that it is.

SEXTON
45   What else, fellow?

FIRST WATCHMAN
And that Count Claudio did mean upon his words to
disgrace Hero before the whole assembly, and not marry
her.

DOGBERRY
(to BORACHIO*)* O villain! Thou wilt be condemned into
50   everlasting redemption for this.

SEXTON
What else?

FIRST WATCHMAN
This is all.

FIRST WATCHMAN

> This man said, sir, that Don John, the Prince's brother, was a villain.

DOGBERRY

Dogberry probably means "treachery" or "slander."

> Write down that Prince John is a villain. Why, that's flat-out perjury—to call a prince's brother a villain.

BORACHIO

> Master Constable—

DOGBERRY

> Be quiet, you. I swear, I don't like the look of you.

SEXTON

> *(to the watchmen)* What else did you hear him say?

SECOND WATCHMAN

> That Don John had given him a thousand pieces of gold for wrongfully accusing the Lady Hero.

DOGBERRY

> That's burglary, that is.

VERGES

> Yes, by God, that it is.

SEXTON

> What else did you hear?

FIRST WATCHMAN

> I heard that Count Claudio meant to disgrace Hero in front of the whole wedding party and refuse to marry her.

DOGBERRY

> *(to* BORACHIO*)* Oh, you villain! You'll be condemned to everlasting redemption for this!

"Redemption" is a mistake for "damnation."

SEXTON

> What else?

FIRST WATCHMAN
> That's all.

SEXTON

And this is more, masters, than you can deny. Prince John
is this morning secretly stolen away. Hero was in this
manner accused, in this very manner refused, and upon the
grief of this, suddenly died.—Master Constable, let these
men be bound and brought to Leonato's. I will go before
and show him their examination.

Exit

DOGBERRY

Come, let them be opinioned.

VERGES

Let them be in the hands—

CONRADE

Off, coxcomb!

DOGBERRY

God's my life, where's the Sexton? Let him write down the
Prince's officer "coxcomb." Come, bind them.—Thou
naughty varlet!

CONRADE

Away! You are an ass, you are an ass!

DOGBERRY

Dost thou not suspect my place? Dost thou not suspect my
years? Oh, that he were here to write me down an ass! But
masters, remember that I am an ass, though it be not
written down, yet forget not that I am an ass.—No, thou
villain, thou art full of piety, as shall be proved upon thee by
good witness. I am a wise fellow and, which is more, an
officer and, which is more, a householder and, which is
more, as pretty a piece of flesh as any is in Messina, and one
that knows the law, go to, and a rich fellow enough, go to,
and a fellow that hath had losses, and one that hath two
gowns and everything handsome about him.—Bring him
away.—Oh, that I had been writ down an ass!

Exeunt

SEXTON

(to CONRADE *and* BORACHIO*)* You can't deny this, gentlemen. This morning, Prince John secretly snuck out of Messina. Hero was accused exactly as the watchman described, and died on the spot from the grief. Master Constable, tie up these men and bring them to Leonato's. I'll get there first and tell him what we found out.

He exits.

DOGBERRY

Come on, let's get them opinioned.

VERGES

Let them be in the hands—

By "opinioned," he means "pinioned" (tied down by the arms).

CONRADE

Get off me, you fool!

DOGBERRY

Honest to God, where's the sexton? He should write down that the Prince's officer was called a fool. Come on, tie them up. *(to* CONRADE*)* You're a nasty little stinker!

CONRADE

Get away from me, you ass! You ass!

DOGBERRY

"Suspect" is a mistake for "respect."

How can you call me that? Don't you suspect my office? Don't you suspect my age? Oh, if only the sexton were here to write down that I'm an ass! Gentlemen, remember that I am an ass; even though it's not written down, don't forget that I'm an ass. Oh, you're a rotten bastard, you are. I'm a wise man and, what's more, I'm an officer of the law and, what's more, I'm a householder and, what's more, I'm as handsome a hunk of meat as any in Messina. And I know the law, damn you, and I'm rich enough, damn you, and I used to have more, but I still have two robes and lots of lovely things.—Take him away!—Oh, if only the sexton had recorded that I'm an ass!

They all exit.

ACT FIVE

SCENE 1

Enter LEONATO *and* ANTONIO

ANTONIO
　　If you go on thus, you will kill yourself,
　　And 'tis not wisdom thus to second grief
　　Against yourself.

LEONATO
　　　　　　　　　　I pray thee, cease thy counsel,
　　Which falls into mine ears as profitless
5　　As water in a sieve. Give not me counsel,
　　Nor let no comforter delight mine ear
　　But such a one whose wrongs do suit with mine.
　　Bring me a father that so loved his child,
　　Whose joy of her is overwhelmed like mine,
10　　And bid him speak of patience.
　　Measure his woe the length and breadth of mine,
　　And let it answer every strain for strain,
　　As thus for thus and such a grief for such,
　　In every lineament, branch, shape, and form.
15　　If such a one will smile and stroke his beard,
　　Bid sorrow wag, cry "hem" when he should groan,
　　Patch grief with proverbs, make misfortune drunk
　　With candle-wasters, bring him yet to me
　　And I of him will gather patience.
20　　But there is no such man. For, brother, men
　　Can counsel and speak comfort to that grief
　　Which they themselves not feel, but, tasting it,
　　Their counsel turns to passion which before
　　Would give preceptial med'cine to rage,
25　　Fetter strong madness in a silken thread,
　　Charm ache with air, and agony with words.

ACT FIVE

SCENE 1

LEONATO *and* ANTONIO *enter.*

ANTONIO

If you keep on the way you've been going, you'll kill yourself. There's no point in adding to your grief.

LEONATO

Stop advising me; your words pass through my ears like water through a sieve. Don't counsel me. Only someone who's been wronged as I have can comfort me. Find a father who loved his child as overwhelmingly as I loved Hero and ask *him* to be patient. Compare the length and width of that man's sadness against my own; match up all the complaints and strong emotions that run through our bodies. If a man who has suffered as I have gave me advice the way you do—smiling and stroking his beard, telling me to toss away my sorrow, giving speeches when he should be wailing with me, trying to heal my grief with little proverbs, spinning my head around with philosophy—then I would take his advice and be patient. But that man doesn't exist. You can try to comfort a man who feels a pain that you have never felt, but once you feel it too, your sober advice will also turn into passion. You can't treat madness with rules or bind up insanity with little silken threads or cure heartache with hot air or lighten agony with pat phrases.

No, no, 'tis all men's office to speak patience
To those that wring under the load of sorrow,
But no man's virtue nor sufficiency
30   To be so moral when he shall endure
The like himself. Therefore give me no counsel.
My griefs cry louder than advertisement.

ANTONIO
Therein do men from children nothing differ.

LEONATO
I pray thee, peace. I will be flesh and blood,
35   For there was never yet philosopher
That could endure the toothache patiently,
However they have writ the style of gods
And made a push at chance and sufferance.

ANTONIO
Yet bend not all the harm upon yourself.
40   Make those that do offend you suffer too.

LEONATO
There thou speak'st reason. Nay, I will do so.
My soul doth tell me Hero is belied,
And that shall Claudio know; so shall the Prince
And all of them that thus dishonor her.

Enter DON PEDRO *and* CLAUDIO

ANTONIO
45   Here comes the Prince and Claudio hastily.

DON PEDRO
Good e'en, good e'en.

CLAUDIO
                              Good day to both of you.

LEONATO
Hear you, my lords—

DON PEDRO
                              We have some haste, Leonato.

Every man thinks it's his duty to advise those who are overwrought with sorrow to be patient. But no man is so moral or so strong that they can endure the same advice when they themselves are grieving. So don't advise me. My sorrow is crying too loudly to hear what you have to say.

ANTONIO

Well then you're no better than a child.

LEONATO

Please, leave me alone. I intend to be flesh and blood, not airy philosophy, for there has never yet been a philosopher who could endure a toothache patiently, even though they all write as if they had risen above human suffering and misfortune.

ANTONIO

But don't take all that pain on yourself. Make sure the ones who have wronged you suffer too.

LEONATO

Now you're talking. I definitely will. In my soul, I believe Hero has been falsely accused. And I'll make sure that Claudio, the Prince, and anyone else who helped dishonor her know about it.

DON PEDRO *and* CLAUDIO *enter.*

ANTONIO

The Prince and Claudio are hurrying this way.

DON PEDRO

Good evening, good evening.

CLAUDIO

Good day to both of you.

LEONATO

Listen, my lords—

DON PEDRO

We're in a bit of a hurry, Leonato.

LEONATO
Some haste, my lord! Well, fare you well, my lord.
Are you so hasty now? Well, all is one.

DON PEDRO
50   Nay, do not quarrel with us, good old man.

ANTONIO
If he could right himself with quarreling,
Some of us would lie low.

CLAUDIO
                            Who wrongs him?

LEONATO
Marry, thou dost wrong me, thou dissembler, thou.
Nay, never lay thy hand upon thy sword.
55   I fear thee not.

CLAUDIO
                        Marry, beshrew my hand
If it should give your age such cause of fear.
In faith, my hand meant nothing to my sword.

LEONATO
Tush, tush, man, never fleer and jest at me.
I speak not like a dotard nor a fool,
60   As under privilege of age to brag
What I have done being young, or what would do
Were I not old. Know, Claudio, to thy head,
Thou hast so wronged mine innocent child and me
That I am forced to lay my reverence by,
65   And with gray hairs and bruise of many days
Do challenge thee to trial of a man.
I say thou hast belied mine innocent child.
Thy slander hath gone through and through her heart,
And she lies buried with her ancestors,
70   Oh, in a tomb where never scandal slept
Save this of hers, framed by thy villainy.

CLAUDIO
My villainy?

LEONATO

A bit of a hurry, my lord! Well then, good bye, my lord. You're in a hurry, are you? Well then, don't bother.

DON PEDRO

Come on, don't quarrel with us, good old man.

ANTONIO

If it's fighting he is after, some of us here should run and hide.

CLAUDIO

Who has wronged him?

LEONATO

Indeed, you have wronged me, you liar. Don't bother trying to intimidate me by putting your hand on your sword. I'm not scared of you.

CLAUDIO

Curse my hand if it ever threatened an old man like you. Really, I had no intention of going for my sword.

LEONATO

Damn you, don't mock and sneer at me. I'm not a doddering old fool who brags about the things he did when he was young, and what he would do now if he weren't so old. Claudio, I'm telling you right to your face that you have wronged me and my innocent child. I am forced to lay aside my old man's respectability, and with my gray hairs and my aching body I challenge you to a duel. You have ruined my innocent child. Your slander has broken her heart, and now she lies buried with her ancestors in a tomb—ancestors who had never been tainted by scandal until you caused one with your wickedness.

CLAUDIO

My wickedness?

LEONATO
                    Thine, Claudio, thine, I say.

DON PEDRO
        You say not right, old man.

LEONATO
                        My lord, my lord,
        I'll prove it on his body if he dare,
75   Despite his nice fence and his active practice,
        His May of youth and bloom of lustihood.

CLAUDIO
        Away! I will not have to do with you.

LEONATO
        Canst thou so daff me? Thou hast killed my child.
        If thou kill'st me, boy, thou shalt kill a man.

ANTONIO
80   He shall kill two of us, and men indeed,
        But that's no matter. Let him kill one first.
        Win me and wear me! Let him answer me.—
        Come, follow me, boy. Come, sir boy, come, follow me.
        Sir boy, I'll whip you from your foining fence,
85   Nay, as I am a gentleman, I will.

LEONATO
        Brother—

ANTONIO
        Content yourself. God knows I loved my niece,
        And she is dead, slandered to death by villains
        That dare as well answer a man indeed
90   As I dare take a serpent by the tongue.—
        Boys, apes, braggarts, jacks, milksops!

LEONATO
        Brother Anthony—

LEONATO

Yours, Claudio, yours, I say.

DON PEDRO

You've got it wrong, old man.

LEONATO

My lord, if he dares to accept my challenge, I'll beat him and prove he's guilty. I'll beat him despite his fancy fencing techniques and all the practicing he does, despite his youth and manliness.

CLAUDIO

Not a chance! I'll have nothing to do with you.

LEONATO

You think you can get rid of me that easily? You killed my child. Take on someone your own size: if you kill me, boy, you'll have killed a man.

ANTONIO

He'll have to kill both of us, and indeed we're both men. But let him start off easy by killing one of us. Come on—kill me and brag about it! Let me at him. Come on, come after me, little boy. Come on and get me. Little man, I'll be right in your face with my sword. I will, as surely as I am a gentleman.

LEONATO

Brother—

ANTONIO

Quiet. God knows I loved my niece, and now she's dead—slandered to death by cowards who would just as likely fight a real man as I would grab a poisonous snake by the tongue. Boys, fools, braggers, scoundrels, babies!

LEONATO

Brother Anthony—

ANTONIO
Hold you content. What, man! I know them, yea,
And what they weigh, even to the utmost scruple—
95 Scrambling, outfacing, fashion-monging boys,
That lie and cog and flout, deprave and slander,
Go anticly and show outward hideousness,
And speak off half a dozen dang'rous words
How they might hurt their enemies, if they durst,
100 And this is all.

LEONATO
But brother Anthony—

ANTONIO
                              Come, 'tis no matter.
Do not you meddle. Let me deal in this.

DON PEDRO
Gentlemen both, we will not wake your patience.
My heart is sorry for your daughter's death,
105 But, on my honor, she was charged with nothing
But what was true and very full of proof.

LEONATO
  · My lord, my lord—

DON PEDRO
I will not hear you.

LEONATO
No? Come, brother; away! I will be heard.

ANTONIO
110 And shall, or some of us will smart for it.

Exeunt LEONATO *and* ANTONIO

Enter BENEDICK

DON PEDRO
See, see, here comes the man we went to seek.

CLAUDIO
Now, Signior, what news?

ANTONIO

Hold your peace. I know their kind, I know them exactly. They're petulant, disrespectful, fashion-crazy boys who lie and cheat and mock, defame and slander. They walk around in outlandish outfits, pretending to be brave and wild and saying a few inflammatory things about how they'll hurt their enemies—and that's all they do.

LEONATO

But brother Anthony—

ANTONIO

Don't, it's no big deal. Don't bother with it. Let me deal with this.

DON PEDRO

Gentlemen, we won't stay here and anger you further. I'm sorry about your daughter's death, but I swear our accusations were true, and backed up with proof.

LEONATO

My lord, my lord—

DON PEDRO

I don't want to hear any more about it.

LEONATO

No? Come on, brother! I'm determined to be heard by someone.

ANTONIO

And you will be, or some people here will suffer for it.

> LEONATO *and* ANTONIO *exit.*
> BENEDICK *enters.*

DON PEDRO

Look, here comes just the man we were looking for.

CLAUDIO

What's up, mister?

BENEDICK
   (to DON PEDRO*)* Good day, my lord.

DON PEDRO
   Welcome, Signior. You are almost come to part almost a
115 fray.

CLAUDIO
   We had like to have had our two noses snapped off with two
   old men without teeth.

DON PEDRO
   Leonato and his brother. What think'st thou? Had we
   fought, I doubt we should have been too young for them.

BENEDICK
120 In a false quarrel there is no true valor. I came to seek you
   both.

CLAUDIO
   We have been up and down to seek thee, for we are high-
   proof melancholy and would fain have it beaten away. Wilt
   thou use thy wit?

BENEDICK
125 It is in my scabbard. Shall I draw it?

DON PEDRO
   Dost thou wear thy wit by thy side?

CLAUDIO
   Never any did so, though very many have been beside their
   wit. I will bid thee draw, as we do the minstrels: draw to
   pleasure us.

DON PEDRO
130 As I am an honest man, he looks pale.—Art thou sick, or
   angry?

CLAUDIO
   (to BENEDICK*)* What, courage, man! What though care
   killed a cat? Thou hast mettle enough in thee to kill care.

BENEDICK

(to DON PEDRO*)* Hello, my lord.

DON PEDRO

Welcome, sir. You just missed a fight that was barely avoided.

CLAUDIO

We were about to have our noses snapped off by two old men with no teeth.

DON PEDRO

Leonato and his brother. What do you think? I think if we had fought, we would have proven too young and strong for them after all.

BENEDICK

There's no bravery in an unfair fight. I've been looking for you two.

CLAUDIO

We've been looking for you, too. We're really depressed. Will you tell us some jokes to beat our sadness away?

BENEDICK

A scabbard is a covering for a sword.

My wit's in my scabbard. Should I unsheath it?

DON PEDRO

You wear your wit next to you?

CLAUDIO

"beside their wit" = crazy

No one carries their wit next to them, though some people are beside their wit. Come on, draw your wit, just as musicians draw their bows across the instruments: draw for our pleasure.

DON PEDRO

Look: Benedick is so pale—are you sick, or angry?

CLAUDIO

"Care" here means "seriousness." Claudio puns on an old proverb.

(to BENEDICK*)* Buck up, man! Care may have killed the cat, but you are strong enough to kill care. Lighten up.

BENEDICK
> Sir, I shall meet your wit in the career, an you charge it
135   against me. I pray you, choose another subject.

CLAUDIO
> *(to* DON PEDRO*)* Nay, then, give him another staff. This last
> was broke 'cross.

DON PEDRO
> By this light, he changes more and more. I think he be angry
> indeed.

CLAUDIO
140   If he be, he knows how to turn his girdle.

BENEDICK
> Shall I speak a word in your ear?

CLAUDIO
> God bless me from a challenge!

BENEDICK
> *(aside to* CLAUDIO*)* You are a villain. I jest not. I will make it
> good how you dare, with what you dare, and when you
145   dare. Do me right, or I will protest your cowardice. You
> have killed a sweet lady, and her death shall fall heavy on
> you. Let me hear from you.

CLAUDIO
> Well, I will meet you, so I may have good cheer.

DON PEDRO
> What, a feast, a feast?

CLAUDIO
150   I' faith, I thank him. He hath bid me to a calf's head and a
> capon, the which if I do not carve most curiously, say my
> knife's naught. Shall I not find a woodcock too?

BENEDICK
> Sir, your wit ambles well; it goes easily.

BENEDICK

Sir, don't even try to beat me in a battle of wits. I'll meet all your attacks, even if you come charging at me with a lance at full gallop. Choose another tack.

CLAUDIO

(to DON PEDRO) That was poor, Benedick! Give him another lance—that last one got broken in half.

DON PEDRO

Lord, he seems to be getting paler by the minute. I think he really is angry.

CLAUDIO

If he is, that's his problem.

BENEDICK

Can I have a word with you privately?

CLAUDIO

God forbid he wants to challenge me!

BENEDICK

(speaking so that only CLAUDIO can hear) You are a villain. I'm not kidding. I challenge you however you like—with whatever weapons you choose, and whenever you want. Meet this challenge, or I'll say that you're a coward. You've killed an innocent woman, and you're going to pay dearly for her death. What do you say?

CLAUDIO

I'll be there, and I'll enjoy myself.

DON PEDRO

What, are we having a feast?

CLAUDIO

Calf's heads, capons, and woodcocks are all dishes that symbolize stupidity.

Yes, we are. He has invited me to have a calf's head and a capon. He says if I don't carve them up and serve them elegantly, he'll declare I have no skills with a knife. Should I go get us a woodcock, too?

BENEDICK

Sir, you have a very slow, rambling wit.

DON PEDRO
I'll tell thee how Beatrice praised thy wit the other day. I
155   said thou hadst a fine wit. "True," said she, "a fine little
one." "No," said I, "a great wit." "Right," says she, "a great
gross one." "Nay," said I, "a good wit." "Just," said she, "it
hurts nobody." "Nay," said I, "the gentleman is wise."
"Certain," said she, "a wise gentleman." "Nay," said I, "he
160   hath the tongues." "That I believe," said she, "for he swore
a thing to me on Monday night, which he forswore on
Tuesday morning; there's a double tongue, there's two
tongues." Thus did she an hour together transshape thy
particular virtues. Yet at last she concluded with a sigh,
165   thou wast the proper'st man in Italy.

CLAUDIO
For the which she wept heartily and said she cared not.

DON PEDRO
Yea, that she did. But yet for all that, an if she did not hate
him deadly, she would love him dearly. The old man's
daughter told us all.

CLAUDIO
170   All, all. And, moreover, God saw him when he was hid in
the garden.

DON PEDRO
But when shall we set the savage bull's horns on the sensible
Benedick's head?

CLAUDIO
Yea, and text underneath: "Here dwells Benedick the
175   married man"?

BENEDICK
Fare you well, boy. You know my mind. I will leave you now
to your gossip-like humor. You break jests as braggarts do
their blades, which, God be thanked, hurt not.—My lord,
for your many courtesies I thank you. I must discontinue
180   your company.

DON PEDRO

Benedick, Beatrice praised your wit the other day. I said you had a fine wit. "True," she said, "a fine little one." "No," I said, "a huge wit." "Right," she said, "a hugely awful one." "No," I said, "he has a good wit." "Exactly," she said, "it's good and mild; it doesn't hurt anyone." "No," I said, "Benedick is wise." "He is certainly," she said, "a wise gentleman." "No," I said, "he can speak many languages:" "I can believe that," she said, "because he swore one thing to me on Monday night and took it back on Tuesday morning. He spoke two languages then." She turned all your virtues into vices just about an hour ago. But in the end she sighed and admitted you were the handsomest man in Italy.

"A wise gentleman" was often used to describe an old, foolish man.

CLAUDIO

She cried a lot at that, and said she didn't care.

DON PEDRO

That she did. And yet for all that, if she didn't hate him to death, she'd love him to death. Leonato's daughter had told us everything.

CLAUDIO

Absolutely everything. And, moreover, God saw Benedick when he was hid in the garden.

DON PEDRO

But when exactly will we see Benedick married?

CLAUDIO

Yes, with the sign underneath him that says: "Here lives Benedick the married man"?

BENEDICK

Goodbye, boy. You know what I intend. I'll leave you now to chatter and gossip like an old woman. The wit you flaunt is like a blunt sword—it can't hurt anyone, thank God.—My lord, I thank you for your many kindnesses. I'm leaving your court now.

Your brother the Bastard is fled from Messina. You have
among you killed a sweet and innocent lady. For my Lord
Lackbeard there, he and I shall meet, and till then peace be
with him.

Exit

DON PEDRO
185   He is in earnest.

CLAUDIO
In most profound earnest, and, I'll warrant you, for the love
of Beatrice.

DON PEDRO
And hath challenged thee?

CLAUDIO
Most sincerely.

DON PEDRO
190   What a pretty thing man is when he goes in his doublet and
hose and leaves off his wit!

CLAUDIO
He is then a giant to an ape; but then is an ape a doctor to
such a man.

DON PEDRO
But soft you, let me be. Pluck up, my heart, and be sad. Did
195   he not say my brother was fled?

Enter DOGBERRY, VERGES, *and the Watch, with* CONRADE
and BORACHIO

DOGBERRY
Come you, sir. If justice cannot tame you, she shall ne'er
weigh more reasons in her balance. Nay, an you be a cursing
hypocrite once, you must be looked to.

DON PEDRO
How now? Two of my brother's men bound! Borachio one!

Your brother Don John the Bastard has run away from Messina. The three of you have killed a sweet, innocent woman. Lord Babyface over there will meet me in a duel, and good luck to him then.

He exits.

DON PEDRO

He's serious.

CLAUDIO

Very serious, and I'm sure it's because of Beatrice.

DON PEDRO

And he challenged you to a duel?

CLAUDIO

He did, very sincerely.

DON PEDRO

What a strange sight—a man who has put on all his fancy clothes but forgotten his brain at home!

CLAUDIO

A guy like that is bigger than an ape, but the ape could be his doctor, it's so much smarter.

DON PEDRO

But wait a minute. Let me gather my wits and get serious here. Didn't he say my brother has run away?

DOGBERRY, VERGES, *and the* WATCHMEN *enter with* CONRADE *and* BORACHIO.

DOGBERRY

Come on, you. If they let you off, then we'll have to assume that Lady Justice has lost all her power. Since you are a lying hypocrite, we must look after you.

DON PEDRO

What's this? Two of my brother's men, all tied up! And Borachio is one of them!

CLAUDIO

200   Hearken after their offense, my lord.

DON PEDRO

Officers, what offense have these men done?

DOGBERRY

Marry, sir, they have committed false report; moreover,
they have spoken untruths; secondarily, they are slanders;
sixth and lastly, they have belied a lady; thirdly, they have
205   verified unjust things; and, to conclude, they are lying
knaves.

DON PEDRO

First, I ask thee what they have done; thirdly, I ask thee
what's their offense; sixth and lastly, why they are
committed; and, to conclude, what you lay to their charge.

CLAUDIO

210   Rightly reasoned, and in his own division; and, by my
troth, there's one meaning well suited.

DON PEDRO

(to BORACHIO *and* CONRADE) Who have you offended,
masters, that you are thus bound to your answer? This
learned constable is too cunning to be understood. What's
215   your offense?

BORACHIO

Sweet Prince, let me go no farther to mine answer. Do you
hear me, and let this count kill me. I have deceived even your
very eyes. What your wisdoms could not discover, these
shallow fools have brought to light, who in the night
220   overheard me confessing to this man how Don John your
brother incensed me to slander the Lady Hero, how you
were brought into the orchard and saw me court Margaret in
Hero's garments, how you disgraced her when you should
marry her. My villainy they have upon record, which I had
225.   rather seal with my death than repeat over to my shame. The
lady is dead upon mine and my master's false accusation.
And, briefly, I desire nothing but the reward of a villain.

CLAUDIO

Find out what they're being held for.

DON PEDRO

Officers, what crime have these men committed?

DOGBERRY

Well sir, they've lied; moreover, they have said things that were not true; secondarily, they are slanderers; sixth and lastly, they have falsely accused a lady; thirdly, they have confirmed things that did not in fact happen; and, in conclusion, they are lying scoundrels.

DON PEDRO

First, I ask you what they've done; thirdly, I ask you what offense they're charged with; sixth and lastly, I ask you why they've been committed here; and, in conclusion, I ask what they're accused of.

CLAUDIO

Nicely done, and organized in just the way he'll understand. My God, he manages to say the same thing six different ways.

DON PEDRO

(to BORACHIO *and* CONRADE*)* What have you done, gentlemen? This educated constable is too brilliant for me to understand. What is your crime?

BORACHIO

Prince, I won't wait for my trial: listen to my story, and let the count kill me now. I tricked your own eyes. These stupid fools have uncovered what you in all your wisdom could not. They heard me confess to Conrade how Don John, your brother, prompted me to slander Hero—how you came to the orchard and saw me making sexual advances toward Margaret, who was disguised as Hero; how you disgraced Hero when you should have married her. They've recorded my crimes, and I would rather die than have to retell this shameful story. The lady has died because of the false accusations of me and my master. I desire nothing now but a criminal's punishment.

DON PEDRO
    (to CLAUDIO*)* Runs not this speech like iron through your
    blood?

CLAUDIO
230. I have drunk poison whiles he uttered it.

DON PEDRO
    (to BORACHIO*)* But did my brother set thee on to this?

BORACHIO
    Yea, and paid me richly for the practice of it.

DON PEDRO
    He is composed and framed of treachery,
    And fled he is upon this villainy.

CLAUDIO
235   Sweet Hero, now thy image doth appear
    In the rare semblance that I loved it first.

DOGBERRY
    Come, bring away the plaintiffs. By this time our sexton
    hath reformed Signior Leonato of the matter. And,
    masters, do not forget to specify, when time and place shall
240   serve, that I am an ass.

VERGES
    Here, here comes Master Signior Leonato, and the Sexton
    too.

    Enter LEONATO *and* ANTONIO, *with the* SEXTON

LEONATO
    Which is the villain? Let me see his eyes,
    That, when I note another man like him,
245   I may avoid him. Which of these is he?

BORACHIO
    If you would know your wronger, look on me.

LEONATO
    Art thou the slave that with thy breath hast killed
    Mine innocent child?

DON PEDRO

(to CLAUDIO*)* Doesn't this make your blood run cold?

CLAUDIO

His words are like poison to me.

DON PEDRO

(to BORACHIO*)* But did my brother prompt you to do all this?

BORACHIO

Yes, and paid me well for doing it.

DON PEDRO

He is made of treachery, and has run away to avoid his crimes.

CLAUDIO

Sweet Hero; when I imagine you now, you seem as beautiful as you did when I first loved you.

DOGBERRY

"Plaintiffs" is a mistake for "defendant"; "reformed" is a mistake for "informed."

Come, take away the plaintiffs. By now the sexton will have reformed Signior Leonato of the matter. *(to* CLAUDIO *and* DON PEDRO*)* And, gentlemen, please do not forget to specify, whenever it is convenient, that I am an ass.

VERGES

Here comes Master Signior Leonato with the sexton.

LEONATO *and* ANTONIO *enter with the* SEXTON.

LEONATO

Which one of them did it? Let me see what he looks like, so when I see another man who resembles him, I'll know to avoid him. Which one is it?

BORACHIO

If you want to see your deceiver, then look at me.

LEONATO

Are you the slave who, with your slanderous words, killed my innocent child?

BORACHIO
Yea, even I alone.

LEONATO
No, not so, villain, thou beliest thyself.
250   Here stand a pair of honorable men—
A third is fled—that had a hand in it.—
I thank you, princes, for my daughter's death.
Record it with your high and worthy deeds.
'Twas bravely done, if you bethink you of it.

CLAUDIO
255   I know not how to pray your patience,
Yet I must speak. Choose your revenge yourself.
Impose me to what penance your invention
Can lay upon my sin. Yet sinned I not
But in mistaking.

DON PEDRO
By my soul, nor I,
260   And yet to satisfy this good old man
I would bend under any heavy weight
That he'll enjoin me to.

LEONATO
I cannot bid you bid my daughter live—
That were impossible—but, I pray you both,
265   Possess the people in Messina here
How innocent she died. And if your love
Can labor ought in sad invention,
Hang her an epitaph upon her tomb
And sing it to her bones. Sing it tonight.
270   Tomorrow morning come you to my house,
And since you could not be my son-in-law,
Be yet my nephew. My brother hath a daughter,
Almost the copy of my child that's dead,
And she alone is heir to both of us.
275   Give her the right you should have given her cousin,
And so dies my revenge.

BORACHIO

Yes, I am the one.

LEONATO

No, villain, but you didn't work alone. *(indicating* CLAUDIO *and* DON PEDRO*)* For here are two noblemen —the third has run away—who helped you. *(to* CLAUDIO *and* DON PEDRO*)* Thank you, gentlemen, for my daughter's death. Make a note of it on your long lists of righteous and worthy deeds. It was very brave of you.

CLAUDIO

I don't know how to ask you for forgiveness, but I have to say something. Choose your revenge. Punish me through any means you can devise, though I sinned by mistake.

DON PEDRO

Me too—but to satisfy this good old man, I too will bear any punishment he gives me.

LEONATO

I can't ask you to make my daughter live—that's impossible—but I beg you both to tell the people of Messina that she was innocent when she died. And if your love can produce something from its sadness, write a poem for her; hang it on her grave and sing it to her bones. Sing it tonight. Then come to my house tomorrow morning, and since you couldn't be my son-in-law, be my nephew instead. My brother has a daughter who looks exactly like Hero; this girl is heir to both our estates. Marry her as you should have married her cousin, and I will let my revenge die.

CLAUDIO
                    O noble sir!
Your overkindness doth wring tears from me.
I do embrace your offer; and dispose
For henceforth of poor Claudio.

LEONATO
280   Tomorrow then I will expect your coming.
Tonight I take my leave. This naughty man
Shall face to face be brought to Margaret,
Who I believe was packed in all this wrong,
Hired to it by your brother.

BORACHIO
285   No, by my soul, she was not,
Nor knew not what she did when she spoke to me,
But always hath been just and virtuous
In any thing that I do know by her.

DOGBERRY
(to LEONATO*)* Moreover, sir, which indeed is not under
290   white and black, this plaintiff here, the offender, did call me
ass. I beseech you, let it be remembered in his punishment.
And also the watch heard them talk of one Deformed. They
say he wears a key in his ear and a lock hanging by it and
borrows money in God's name, the which he hath used so
295   long and never paid that now men grow hard-hearted and
will lend nothing for God's sake. Pray you, examine him
upon that point.

LEONATO
I thank thee for thy care and honest pains.

DOGBERRY
Your worship speaks like a most thankful and reverent
300   youth, and I praise God for you.

LEONATO
(giving him money) There's for thy pains.

CLAUDIO

Oh, noble sir! Your overwhelming kindness makes me weep. I willingly accept your offer and put my future in your hands.

LEONATO

I will see you tomorrow, then. Now I have to leave. This wicked man will be brought face to face with Margaret, who I believe was hired by Don John to take part in this plot.

BORACHIO

No, she wasn't, and she didn't know anything about it. She has always been honest and good.

DOGBERRY

"Plaintiff" is a mistake for "defendant."

Dogberry garbles the events of Act 3, scene 3.

(*to* LEONATO) Also, sir, this hasn't been put down in writing, but I should let you know that this plaintiff here, the criminal, did in fact call me an ass. Please remember that when you're punishing him. Plus, the watchmen heard the criminals talking about some man named Deformed. They say that he has an earring made out of a key, with a lock hanging from it. Apparently, he borrows money from people in the name of God and then never pays it back, which angers everyone so much that they now refuse to fund anything in the name of God. Make sure you ask him about this.

LEONATO

Thank you for all your efforts.

DOGBERRY

You speak like a very thankful and respectful boy, and may God bless you.

LEONATO

(*giving* DOGBERRY *money*) This is for your trouble.

DOGBERRY
God save the foundation!

LEONATO
Go, I discharge thee of thy prisoner, and I thank thee.

DOGBERRY
I leave an arrant knave with your Worship, which I beseech
305   your Worship to correct yourself, for the example of others.
God keep your Worship! I wish your Worship well. God
restore you to health! I humbly give you leave to depart, and
if a merry meeting may be wished, God prohibit it!—
Come, neighbor.

Exeunt DOGBERRY *and* VERGES

LEONATO
310   Until tomorrow morning, lords, farewell.

ANTONIO
Farewell, my lords. We look for you tomorrow.

DON PEDRO
We will not fail.

CLAUDIO
Tonight I'll mourn with Hero.

LEONATO
(to the Watch)
Bring you these fellows on.—We'll talk with Margaret,
315   How her acquaintance grew with this lewd fellow.

Exeunt

DOGBERRY

God save the charitable organization!

LEONATO

Go, you're relieved of your duty. Thank you.

DOGBERRY

I leave a slimy bastard with you, your Worship, for you to punish and make an example of. God bless your Worship! I wish you well. I hope that God restores you to health. I will humbly let you go now, God prohibiting we will meet again in the future.— Come on, man.

"Prohibiting" is a mistake for "permitting."

DOGBERRY *and* VERGES *exit.*

LEONATO

I'll see you tomorrow morning, gentlemen.

ANTONIO

Goodbye, gentlemen. We'll see you tomorrow.

DON PEDRO

We'll be there.

CLAUDIO

I will mourn Hero tonight.

LEONATO

(to the watchmen) Bring these criminals with us. We'll go talk to Margaret, to see how she got involved with this worthless man.

They all exit.

ACT 5, SCENE 2

Enter BENEDICK *and* MARGARET

BENEDICK
Pray thee, sweet Mistress Margaret, deserve well at my
hands by helping me to the speech of Beatrice.

MARGARET
Will you then write me a sonnet in praise of my beauty?

BENEDICK
In so high a style, Margaret, that no man living shall come
5   over it, for in most comely truth thou deservest it.

MARGARET
To have no man come over me! Why, shall I always keep
below stairs?

BENEDICK
Thy wit is as quick as the greyhound's mouth; it catches.

MARGARET
And yours as blunt as the fencer's foils, which hit but hurt
10   not.

BENEDICK
A most manly wit, Margaret, it will not hurt a woman. And
so, I pray thee, call Beatrice. I give thee the bucklers.

MARGARET
Give us the swords; we have bucklers of our own.

BENEDICK
If you use them, Margaret, you must put in the pikes with
15   a vice, and they are dangerous weapons for maids.

MARGARET
Well, I will call Beatrice to you, who I think hath legs.

ACT 5, SCENE 2

BENEDICK *and* MARGARET *enter.*

BENEDICK

Please Margaret, help me write this poem for Beatrice.

MARGARET

Afterward, will you write a sonnet for me, praising my beauty?

BENEDICK

Benedick means that no man will ever improve on his sonnet;

I'll write you such a glorious sonnet, Margaret, that no man will ever be able to come over it. You certainly deserve it.

MARGARET

Margaret interprets "come over" in a sexual way

No man will come over me! What a life that would be!

BENEDICK

Your wit is as quick as a greyhound's jaws—it catches whatever it goes after.

MARGARET

And your wit is as blunt as a practice sword, with its dull tip; it hits people but doesn't hurt them.

BENEDICK

A "buckler" is a shield with a spike in the middle of it.

It's just that my wit is very gentlemanly, Margaret, and refuses to hurt a woman. Now please, tell Beatrice to come out. I admit defeat; I give you the bucklers.

MARGARET

Margaret interprets "buckler" as the vagina (and the sword as the penis).

No, you should give a woman your sword—we have our own bucklers!

BENEDICK

Watch out, though, Margaret—virgins shouldn't be brandishing their bucklers around.

MARGARET

I'll go get Beatrice for you, who can walk here by herself—she has legs.

BENEDICK
And therefore will come.

Exit MARGARET

(sings)
> The god of love,
> That sits above,
20 > And knows me, and knows me,
> How pitiful I deserve—

I mean in singing. But in loving, Leander the good
swimmer, Troilus the first employer of panders, and a
whole bookful of these quondam carpetmongers, whose
25   names yet run smoothly in the even road of a blank verse,
why, they were never so truly turned over and over as my
poor self in love. Marry, I cannot show it in rhyme. I have
tried. I can find out no rhyme to "lady" but "baby"—an
innocent rhyme; for "scorn," "horn"—a hard rhyme; for,
30   "school," "fool"—a babbling rhyme; very ominous
endings. No, I was not born under a rhyming planet, nor I
cannot woo in festival terms.

Enter BEATRICE

Sweet Beatrice, wouldst thou come when I called thee?

BEATRICE
Yea, Signior, and depart when you bid me.

BENEDICK
35   Oh , stay but till then!

BEATRICE
"Then" is spoken. Fare you well now. And yet, ere I go, let
me go with that I came, which is, with knowing what hath
passed between you and Claudio.

BENEDICK
Only foul words, and thereupon I will kiss thee.

BENEDICK

So that means she'll come.

MARGARET exits.

(*singing*)
> The god of love
> He sits in heaven above
> And he knows me, he knows me
> He knows how much pity I deserve—

I'm really a pitiful singer. But as a lover, well, that's another story. Take Leander, Troilus, or an entire book's worth of those legendary lover–boys, whose names sound so smooth and nice in a line of verse— not one of them has been driven as crazy by love as I have been. But I can't prove it in a poem. I have tried. I can't think of any rhyme for "lady" but "baby," which is a childish rhyme. The only rhyme for "scorn" I can come up with is "horn"—a bit off for a love poem. Nothing rhymes with "school" but "fool," and that's a ridiculous jingle. These are all very unpromising line endings. No, I wasn't destined to be a poet, and I can't woo a lady with pretty words.

Leander and Troilus are figures from two separate love stories, both well-known to Shakespeare's audience.

In Shakespeare's time, "horns" were associated with adultery.

BEATRICE enters.

Beatrice, have you come because I called for you?

BEATRICE

Yes, sir, and I'll leave when you ask me to.

BENEDICK

Oh, well, stay till then!

BEATRICE

There—you said "then." So I'll leave now. But before I go, let me get what I came for. What happened between you and Claudio?

BENEDICK

I spoke angry, foul words to him, and with that I will kiss you.

BEATRICE

40   Foul words is but foul wind, and foul wind is but foul breath, and foul breath is noisome. Therefore I will depart unkissed.

BENEDICK

    Thou hast frighted the word out of his right sense, so forcible is thy wit. But I must tell thee plainly, Claudio

45   undergoes my challenge, and either I must shortly hear from him, or I will subscribe him a coward. And I pray thee now tell me, for which of my bad parts didst thou first fall in love with me?

BEATRICE

    For them all together, which maintained so politic a state of

50   evil that they will not admit any good part to intermingle with them. But for which of my good parts did you first suffer love for me?

BENEDICK

    Suffer love! A good epithet! I do suffer love indeed, for I love thee against my will.

BEATRICE

55   In spite of your heart, I think. Alas, poor heart, if you spite it for my sake, I will spite it for yours, for I will never love that which my friend hates.

BENEDICK

    Thou and I are too wise to woo peaceably.

BEATRICE

    It appears not in this confession. There's not one wise man

60   among twenty that will praise himself.

BENEDICK

    An old, an old instance, Beatrice, that lived in the lime of good neighbors. If a man do not erect in this age his own tomb ere he dies, he shall live no longer in monument than the bell rings and the widow weeps.

BEATRICE

65   And how long is that, think you?

BEATRICE

If you had foul words in your mouth, then your breath must be foul, and foul breath is nauseating. Thus, I'll leave without being kissed.

BENEDICK

Your wit is so forceful, it frightens the very meaning out of your words. But I will tell you this very plainly: I have challenged Claudio, and either he'll accept the challenge or admit he's a coward. Now, tell me— which of my bad qualities did you fall in love with first?

BEATRICE

With all of them at once: they work together to create such an entirely evil person that no good ever manages to enter the mix. But tell me—which of my good qualities first made you suffer love for me?

BENEDICK

Suffer love! That's a good way of putting it. I do suffer love, because I love you against my will.

BEATRICE

You love me in spite of your heart, I think. If you spite your heart for my sake, then I will spite it for yours. I will never love the thing my friend hates.

BENEDICK

You and I are too wise to woo each other peacefully.

BEATRICE

It's said that no truly wise man will praise himself. If you say that you are wise, it's likely you're not.

BENEDICK

That's an old proverb, Beatrice, from the time when neighbors praised each other. In this day and age, if a man doesn't erect his own monument before he dies, he won't be remembered past the funeral bell's ringing and his widow's crying.

BEATRICE

Exactly how long is that, do you think?

BENEDICK
Question: why, an hour in clamor and a quarter in rheum.
Therefore is it most expedient for the wise, if Don Worm,
his conscience, find no impediment to the contrary, to be
the trumpet of his own virtues, as I am to myself. So much
70   for praising myself, who, I myself will bear witness, is
praiseworthy. And now tell me, how doth your cousin?

BEATRICE
Very ill.

BENEDICK
And how do you?

BEATRICE
Very ill, too.

BENEDICK
75   Serve God, love me, and mend. There will I leave you too,
for here comes one in haste.

Enter URSULA

URSULA
Madam, you must come to your uncle. Yonder's old coil at
home. It is proved my Lady Hero hath been falsely
accused, the Prince and Claudio mightily abused, and Don
80   John is the author of all, who is fled and gone. Will you
come presently?

Exit

BEATRICE
Will you go hear this news, Signior?

BENEDICK
I will live in thy heart, die in thy lap, and be buried in thy
eyes—and moreover, I will go with thee to thy uncle's.

Exeunt

BENEDICK

About an hour for the ringing and fifteen minutes for the crying. That's why it's better for wise men to trumpet their own virtues, like I do. That's why I praise myself, who—if I do say so myself—is quite praiseworthy. But tell me, how is your cousin?

BEATRICE

She's very sick.

BENEDICK

And how are you?

BEATRICE

I'm very sick, too.

BENEDICK

Have faith, love me, and you will get better. And that's where I'll end, because someone is hurrying this way.

URSULA *enters.*

URSULA

Madam, you have to go to your uncle's. There's a huge racket going on there. It's been proven that Lady Hero is innocent, that the Prince and Claudio have been utterly deceived, and that Don John—who has run away—is the source of all the trouble. Will you come immediately?

She exits.

BEATRICE

Will you come with me to hear this news, sir?

BENEDICK

I will live in your heart, die in your lap, and be buried in your eyes—and, what's more, I will go with you to your uncle's.

They exit.

ACT 5, SCENE 3

Enter DON PEDRO, CLAUDIO, *three or four* LORDS *with tapers, and musicians*

CLAUDIO
Is this the monument of Leonato?

FIRST LORD
It is, my lord.

CLAUDIO
(reading an epitaph)

Done to death by slanderous tongues
Was the Hero that here lies.
5   Death, in guerdon of her wrongs,
Gives her fame which never dies.
So the life that died with shame
Lives in death with glorious fame.

Hangs the scroll

Hang thou there upon the tomb,
10   Praising her when I am dumb.
Now, music, sound, and sing your solemn hymn.

(Song)
     Pardon, goddess of the night,
     Those that slew thy virgin knight,
     For the which with songs of woe
15   *Round about her tomb they go.*
     Midnight, assist our moan.
     Help us to sigh and groan
     Heavily, heavily.
     Graves, yawn and yield your dead,
20   *Till death be utterèd,*
     Heavily, heavily.

ACT 5, SCENE 3

DON PEDRO *and* CLAUDIO *enter with three or four* LORDS *carrying candles, and musicians.*

CLAUDIO

Is this the family tomb of Leonato?

FIRST LORD

It is, my lord.

CLAUDIO

(reading an epitaph)

Here lies Hero,
The heroic maiden killed by slanderous words.
To repay her for her troubles, Death
Gives her undying fame.
So the life that died with shame
Lives on with fame.

(he hangs the scroll)

This epitaph will hang here forever,
Continuing to praise Hero after I die.
Now start the music, and sing the solemn hymn.

Diana was the Roman goddess associated with the moon, and her "knights" were virgin women.

(singing)

Please pardon, goddess of the night,
The men who killed your virgin knight.
These men now walk around her tomb,
Singing songs of woe.
Oh, midnight, join our moaning
Help us with our sighs and groaning
Heavily, heavily.
Graves, open up and release your corpses
Until Hero's death is fully mourned,
Heavily, heavily.

The meaning of this final line is unclear; it may also be interpreted as, "until death itself is beaten," or "until we have fully realized what this death means."

CLAUDIO
> Now, unto thy bones good night!
> Yearly will I do this rite.

DON PEDRO
> Good morrow, masters. Put your torches out.
25   The wolves have preyed, and look, the gentle day,
> Before the wheels of Phoebus, round about
> Dapples the drowsy east with spots of grey.
> Thanks to you all, and leave us. Fare you well.

CLAUDIO
> Good morrow, masters. Each his several way.

Exeunt LORDS *and Musicians*

DON PEDRO
30   Come, let us hence, and put on other weeds,
> And then to Leonato's we will go.

CLAUDIO
> And Hymen now with luckier issue speed 's
> Than this for whom we rendered up this woe.

Exeunt

CLAUDIO

Now I say good night to your bones, Hero. I will perform this ceremony every year.

DON PEDRO

Good morning, gentlemen. Put out your torches. The wolves have finished preying for the night, and look— the gentle dawn is rising, dappling the sleepy eastern sky with spots of light.

CLAUDIO

Good morning, gentlemen. We go our separate ways.

LORDS *and musicians exit.*

DON PEDRO

Come, let's go and change our clothes. Then we'll visit Leonato's.

CLAUDIO

Hymen was the god of marriage.

And I hope Hymen will give us better luck than Hero got.

They all exit.

ACT 5, SCENE 4

Enter LEONATO, ANTONIO, BENEDICK, BEATRICE,
MARGARET, URSULA, FRIAR FRANCIS, *and* HERO

FRIAR FRANCIS
Did I not tell you she was innocent?

LEONATO
So are the Prince and Claudio, who accused her
Upon the error that you heard debated.
But Margaret was in some fault for this,
5   Although against her will, as it appears
In the true course of all the question.

ANTONIO
Well, I am glad that all things sort so well.

BENEDICK
And so am I, being else by faith enforced
To call young Claudio to a reckoning for it.

LEONATO
10   Well, daughter, and you gentlewomen all,
Withdraw into a chamber by yourselves,
And when I send for you, come hither masked.
The Prince and Claudio promised by this hour
To visit me.—You know your office, brother.
15   You must be father to your brother's daughter,
And give her to young Claudio.

Exeunt Ladies

ANTONIO
Which I will do with confirmed countenance.

BENEDICK
Friar, I must entreat your pains, I think.

FRIAR FRANCIS
To do what, Signior?

ACT 5, SCENE 4

LEONATO, ANTONIO, BENEDICK, BEATRICE, MARGARET, URSULA, FRIAR FRANCIS, *and* HERO *enter.*

FRIAR FRANCIS
Didn't I tell you she was innocent?

LEONATO
And the Prince and Claudio, who accused her, are innocent as well, because they were deceived by Don John. Margaret is partially guilty, although our investigation shows that she acted unintentionally.

ANTONIO
Well, I'm glad that everything has been sorted out.

BENEDICK
Me too—otherwise I would have had to duel with Claudio.

LEONATO
Hero, you and the other women should all retreat to a room. When I send for you, come out wearing masks. The Prince and Claudio are supposed to be here by now.—You know your job, brother. You have to pretend to be your niece's father, and give her away to Claudio.

The ladies exit.

ANTONIO
I'll do that, without giving away our secret.

BENEDICK
Friar, I think I need a favor from you.

FRIAR FRANCIS
What do you need me to do?

BENEDICK

20   To bind me or undo me, one of them.—
          Signior Leonato, truth it is, good Signior,
          Your niece regards me with an eye of favor.

LEONATO

          That eye my daughter lent her; 'tis most true.

BENEDICK

          And I do with an eye of love requite her.

LEONATO

25   The sight whereof I think you had from me,
          From Claudio and the Prince. But what's your will?

BENEDICK

          Your answer, sir, is enigmatical.
          But for my will, my will is your goodwill
          May stand with ours, this day to be conjoined
30   In the state of honorable marriage—
          In which, good Friar, I shall desire your help.

LEONATO

          My heart is with your liking.

FRIAR FRANCIS

                                              And my help.
          Here comes the Prince and Claudio.

          Enter DON PEDRO *and* CLAUDIO, *and two or three others*

DON PEDRO

          Good morrow to this fair assembly.

LEONATO

35   Good morrow, Prince; good morrow, Claudio.
          We here attend you. Are you yet determined
          Today to marry with my brother's daughter?

CLAUDIO

          I'll hold my mind were she an Ethiope.

BENEDICK

To tie me up, or to undo me: one or the other. Signior Leonato, the truth is, your niece likes me.

LEONATO

She sees you with the eyes my daughter lent her, it's true.

BENEDICK

And I see her also through the eyes of love.

LEONATO

And those eyes were endowed with sight by Claudio, the Prince, and me. But what did you want?

BENEDICK

Sir, I'm puzzled by what you just said. But as far as what I want—I want you to give Beatrice and me your blessing to be married. That, good Friar, is where you come in.

LEONATO

Our wishes are aligned, then: I give you my blessing.

FRIAR FRANCIS

And I'll help you. Here comes the Prince and Claudio.

DON PEDRO *and* CLAUDIO *enter with two or three others.*

DON PEDRO

Good morning to all these lovely people.

LEONATO

Good morning, Prince; good morning, Claudio. We're waiting here for you. Are you still set on marrying my brother's daughter?

CLAUDIO

Maidens in Shakespeare's time were valued for fair skin. ("Ethiopian" referred to black Africans generally, not to a specific country.)

I wouldn't change my mind even if she were black-skinned.

LEONATO
Call her forth, brother. Here's the friar ready.

Exit ANTONIO

DON PEDRO
40 Good morrow, Benedick. Why, what's the matter
That you have such a February face,
So full of frost, of storm and cloudiness?

CLAUDIO
I think he thinks upon the savage bull.
Tush, fear not, man. We'll tip thy horns with gold,
45 And all Europa shall rejoice at thee
As once Europa did at lusty Jove
When he would play the noble beast in love.

BENEDICK
Bull Jove, sir, had an amiable low,
And some such strange bull leapt your father's cow
50 And got a calf in that same noble feat
Much like to you, for you have just his bleat.

CLAUDIO
For this I owe you. Here comes other reck'nings.

Enter ANTONIO, HERO, BEATRICE, MARGARET, URSULA, *the ladies masked*

Which is the lady I must seize upon?

LEONATO
This same is she, and I do give you her.

CLAUDIO
55 Why, then she's mine.—Sweet, let me see your face.

LEONATO
No, that you shall not till you take her hand
Before this friar and swear to marry her.

LEONATO

Bring her out, brother. The friar's ready.

ANTONIO exits.

DON PEDRO

Good morning, Benedick. What's the matter? Your face looks like the month of February—full of frost, storms, and cloudiness.

CLAUDIO

Claudio continues the jokes of Act 1, scene 1, about husbands and cuckolds' horns.

I think he's nervous—he's about to become the savage bull who got domesticated. Oh, don't worry about it—we'll dip your horns in gold and make you pretty, and you'll delight all of Europe, just like Jove delighted Europa when *he* was a bull.

BENEDICK

The god Jove came to earth in the shape of a bull and carried off the woman Europa.

Jove came to earth lowing for love. A strange bull just like him mated with one of your father's cows and, voilà, gave birth to a calf like you—you bleat the same as him.

CLAUDIO

I'll get you for that one. But here are other matters to be dealt with.

ANTONIO, HERO, BEATRICE, MARGARET, URSULA enter. The ladies wear masks.

Which is the lady I'm supposed to marry?

LEONATO

This one, and I will give her to you.

CLAUDIO

Well, then she's the one for me. Sweetheart, let me see your face.

LEONATO

No, you can't do that until you take her hand and, in front of this friar, swear to marry her.

CLAUDIO
(to HERO) Give me your hand before this holy friar.
I am your husband, if you like of me.

HERO
60 And when I lived, I was your other wife,
And when you loved, you were my other husband.
(She unmasks)

CLAUDIO
Another Hero!

HERO
                              Nothing certainer.
One Hero died defiled, but I do live,
And surely as I live, I am a maid.

DON PEDRO
65 The former Hero! Hero that is dead!

LEONATO
She died, my lord, but whiles her slander lived.

FRIAR FRANCIS
All this amazement can I qualify
When after that the holy rites are ended
I'll tell you largely of fair Hero's death.
70 Meantime let wonder seem familiar,
And to the chapel let us presently.

BENEDICK
Soft and fair, Friar.—Which is Beatrice?

BEATRICE
(unmasking) I answer to that name. What is your will?

BENEDICK
Do not you love me?

BEATRICE
                              Why no, no more than reason.

BENEDICK
75 Why then, your uncle and the Prince and Claudio
Have been deceived. They swore you did.

BEATRICE
Do not you love me?

CLAUDIO

(to HERO*)* Give me your hand. With the friar as my witness, I am your husband, if you want me.

HERO

And when I lived, I was your other wife. And when you loved me, you were my other husband. *(she removes her mask)*

CLAUDIO

It's another Hero!

HERO

Exactly right. One Hero died when she was slandered, but I am alive. And as surely as I am alive, I am a virgin.

DON PEDRO

It's the former Hero! The Hero that died!

LEONATO

She was only dead, my lord, as long as her slander lived.

FRIAR FRANCIS

I can confirm that all these shocking things are true. After the wedding ceremony, I'll tell you all about beautiful Hero's "death." In the meantime, just accept all these wonderful things, and let's head to the chapel.

BENEDICK

Wait a moment, Friar. Which one of you is Beatrice?

BEATRICE

(taking off her mask) That's my name. What do you want?

BENEDICK

Do you love me?

BEATRICE

No, no more than is reasonable.

BENEDICK

Well then, your uncle and the Prince and Claudio have been deceived. They swore you did.

BEATRICE

Do you love me?

BENEDICK
Troth, no, no more than reason.

BEATRICE
Why then, my cousin, Margaret, and Ursula
80   Are much deceived, for they did swear you did.

BENEDICK
They swore that you were almost sick for me.

BEATRICE
They swore that you were well-nigh dead for me.

BENEDICK
'Tis no such matter. Then you do not love me?

BEATRICE
No, truly, but in friendly recompense.

LEONATO
85   Come, cousin, I am sure you love the gentleman.

CLAUDIO
And I'll be sworn upon 't that he loves her,
For here's a paper written in his hand,
A halting sonnet of his own pure brain,
Fashioned to Beatrice.
(Shows a paper)

HERO
                              And here's another,
90   Writ in my cousin's hand, stol'n from her pocket,
Containing her affection unto Benedick.
(Shows a paper)

BENEDICK
A miracle! Here's our own hands against our hearts. Come,
I will have thee, but, by this light, I take thee for pity.

BEATRICE
I would not deny you, but, by this good day, I yield upon
95   great persuasion, and partly to save your life, for I was told
you were in a consumption.

BENEDICK
Peace! I will stop your mouth.

BENEDICK

Truly, no—no more than is reasonable.

BEATRICE

Well then, Margaret, Ursula, and my cousin have been very much deceived, for they swore you did.

BENEDICK

They swore that you were sick with love for me.

BEATRICE

They swore that you were nearly dead with love for me.

BENEDICK

Oh, well. So you don't love me?

BEATRICE

No, I don't—except as a friend.

LEONATO

Come on, niece, I'm sure you love him.

CLAUDIO

And I'll swear that he loves her. Here's a clumsy sonnet, in Benedick's handwriting, dedicated to Beatrice. *(holding up a piece of paper)*

HERO

And here's another poem, which I stole from my cousin's pocket—in her handwriting and all about her adoration for Benedick. *(holding up a piece of paper)*

BENEDICK

What a miracle! Our handwriting gives away our hearts. Come on, I'll take you, but honestly I'm only doing it out of pity.

BEATRICE

I won't say no to you, but let it be known that I'm only doing this after a lot of persuasion and to save your life —I hear you were quickly wasting away without me.

BENEDICK

Oh, shut up! I'll stop your mouth with a kiss.

They kiss

DON PEDRO
How dost thou, Benedick, the married man?

BENEDICK
I'll tell thee what, Prince: a college of wit-crackers cannot
flout me out of my humor. Dost thou think I care for a satire
or an epigram? No. If a man will be beaten with brains, he
shall wear nothing handsome about him. In brief, since I do
purpose to marry, I will think nothing to any purpose that
the world can say against it, and therefore never flout at me
for what I have said against it. For man is a giddy thing, and
this is my conclusion.—For thy part, Claudio, I did think to
have beaten thee, but in that thou art like to be my kinsman,
live unbruised, and love my cousin.

CLAUDIO
I had well hoped thou wouldst have denied Beatrice, that I
might have cudgeled thee out of thy single life, to make thee
a double-dealer, which out of question, thou wilt be, if my
cousin do not look exceedingly narrowly to thee.

BENEDICK
Come, come, we are friends. Let's have a dance ere we are
married, that we may lighten our own hearts and our wives'
heels.

LEONATO
We'll have dancing afterward.

BENEDICK
First, of my word! Therefore play, music.—Prince, thou art
sad. Get thee a wife, get thee a wife. There is no staff more
reverend than one tipped with horn.

Enter a MESSENGER

They kiss.

DON PEDRO

How does it feel to be Benedick the Married Man?

BENEDICK

I'll tell you what, Prince: a whole university full of wisecrackers couldn't change my mood today. You think I care what I'm called? Well, I don't. If a man is always afraid of what others think, he won't even dare to dress nicely, because he'll be afraid people will talk about him. In short, since I intend to get married, I won't hear anyone say a bad thing about it. So don't go making fun of me for what I said before. Man is a giddy, flighty thing: that's my conclusion. And Claudio—though I'm sure I would have beaten you in our duel—since you're likely to become my relative, I'll let you go, unbruised, and love my cousin Hero.

CLAUDIO

I was sort of hoping you would say no to Beatrice, so that I could have smacked you out of your single life and made you a double dealer. Which you'll probably turn into anyway, if my cousin Beatrice doesn't keep you on a short leash.

Here, "double dealer" means both married man and adulterer.

BENEDICK

Come on, we're all friends. Let's do a dance, and have some fun, before we're wed.

LEONATO

We'll dance after the wedding.

BENEDICK

Again, Benedick plays with the idea of the married man as a "horned" cuckold.

No, before! Musicians, play us a song.—Prince, you look sad. You should get a wife! Your royal staff would be so much more impressive if it were topped off by a horn.

A **MESSENGER** *enters.*

MESSENGER
120   *(to* DON PEDRO*)* My lord, your brother John is ta'en in flight
        And brought with armed men back to Messina.

BENEDICK
        (to DON PEDRO*)* Think not on him till tomorrow. I'll devise
        thee brave punishments for him.—Strike up, pipers.

Dance

Exeunt

MESSENGER

> *(to* DON PEDRO*)* My lord, your brother John was caught by armed soldiers as he fled. He's been brought back to Messina.

BENEDICK

> *(to* DON PEDRO*)* Leave him till tomorrow. I'll think of some awful punishment for him. Play on, musicians!

They all dance.

They all exit.

SPARKNOTES LITERATURE GUIDES

Notes

Notes

Notes

Notes